Ariana's Biology

Second edition

The A Level Biologist
your hub

As seen on:

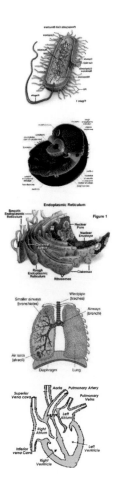

Ariana's AS-level Biology

Ariana Mirzarafie-Ahi

createspace, an Amazon company

www.createspace.com

ISBN-13: 978-1512051957

ISBN-10: 1512051950

Printed in the USA

First published on The A level Biologist – Your Hub (www.thealevelbiologist.co.uk) in 2011, and as an Amazon Kindle eBook in 2013.

eBooks and on demand books published via createspace are environmentally friendly compared to paperbacks printed en masse before being sold.

All efforts have been carried out in tracing picture copyright holders. If any have been overlooked, please contact the author in order to ensure acknowledgement in future editions.

This book is dedicated to the tens of thousands of students taking A-level biology every year in the UK.

AS-level

Contents

Part I

1. Pathogens..6
2. Lifestyle...6
3. The Digestive System...8
4. Proteins...9
5. Enzyme Action...10
6. Enzyme properties..12
7. Carbohydrate Digestion..17
8. Cells..19
9. Plasma Membranes...26
10. Diffusion...29
11. Osmosis..31
12. Active Transport..32
13. Absorption...32
14. Cholera...33
15. Lung Function..35
16. The Biological Basis of Lung Disease...38
17. Heart Structure and Function...40
18. The Biological Basis of Heart Disease..42
19. Principles of Immunology...44

Part II

20. Investigating Variation...48
21. Causes of Variation..50
22. Structure of DNA...51
23. Genes and Polypeptides...54
24. DNA and Chromosomes...56
25. Meiosis...58
26. Genetic Diversity...63
27. Haemoglobin..65
28. Carbohydrates...68
29. Cells..70
30. Replication of DNA...72
31. Mitosis...74
32. Cell Cycle..79
33. Cell Differentiation...81
34. Size and Surface Area..83
35. Gas Exchange..85
36. Mass Transport..90
37. The Blood System...90
38. The Passage of Water through a Plant..................................95
39. Principles of Taxonomy...97
40. Genetic Comparisons...100
41. Courtship Behaviour..102
42. Antibiotics..103
43. Genetic Variation in Bacteria..104
44. Species Diversity..108
45. Index of Diversity..109

Introduction

I was an A-level biology student. Despite countless textbooks, revision guides and websites, I felt alone in my learning quest. It was a stressful time, but I achieved an A. Still, I missed my UCAS university offers. I felt I had let myself down. This is how The A Level Biologist was born.

I say, if the voice of a particular book doesn't reach you, and it's likely it won't, try another voice. The A Level Biologist is your new voice. I wrote the topics based on the AQA exam board specification which is mostly identical to the Edexcel and OCR ones (big hugs to the WJEC and CCEA people). The entire learning environment comprised of your teacher if you have one, textbooks and odd websites is sadly impersonal.

I want to walk you through the biology in my mind. The hope is that your mind will welcome this book as a software installation which can infect it more effectively than others. When I was a kid I had just one general science book. It was fascinating and precious. I read it many times because it was the only one I had.

I want you to look at this book and imagine you are me back then. You have just discovered that on a dusty shelf, too high to reach before, there had been waiting a brand new science book. If you read it as keenly and as often as I read my first science book, you can put those biology exams right to the back of your mind.

I first wrote these notes on The A Level Biologist website. I figured they might benefit greatly from being curated into a book format, and published them on Amazon Kindle. They demanded a book cover, so I made one on the spot. Yes, I made it in Microsoft Paint. Yes, it is fabulous, thank you.

I look forward to getting in touch with you (writing a book as a reply to another book is perhaps too time-consuming, although if it tickles your fancy, please feel free do to it) on The A Level Biologist website, social media especially YouTube where I make videos to complement the other resources such as this book.

I know they say not to begin each paragraph with "I", but they are not part of this. This is between me and you. It's an intimate mental connection and journey. You've got A levels to be getting on with, and I've got a PhD. Ta-ta!

Part I

Pathogens

Pathogens are microorganisms which can cause disease. These include bacteria, viruses and fungi. Have a look at the little things!

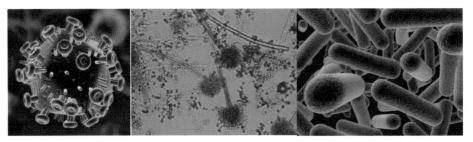

HIV virus, pathogenic fungi and bacteria

(Did you know viruses aren't actually "alive"? They're more like seeds - they multiply under certain conditions, but otherwise, they're dead.)

Pathogens can cause disease when they invade the interface between organisms and their environment. This could be someone's skin, lungs, digestive system, etc.

There are two ways in which pathogens cause disease that you need to know about: 1) damage to the cells, and 2) producing toxins.

Lifestyle

Apart from specific, easily identifiable pathogens such as bacteria or viruses which can cause disease, another major cause of disease is lifestyle. Lifestyle includes the choices that we make in regards to our food, drink, whether we smoke or use drugs, certain jobs we do, even the place where we live.

The way we can measure the impact of certain lifestyle choices is by knowing risk factors. Certain diseases like cancer and coronary heart disease are associated with certain risk factors, such as smoking and obesity. On the flip side, changes in lifestyle are also associated with a decrease in risk of contracting these diseases.

You should be able to analyse graphs showing specific risk factors, such as age, sex or smoking against the incidence of disease such as lung cancer or heart disease. Fetch your textbook and answer those graph questions. Pay special attention to correlations and causations i.e. when a risk factor is associated with a disease, as opposed to when a risk factor causes a disease.

For example, studies over a long period of time have shown that in fact excessive smoking causes lung cancer. On the other hand, living in urban areas is associated with an increased risk of having asthma - this does not mean living in a city causes asthma. Rather, it means it is more likely a city will be more polluted than the countryside, and it is the chemicals in the air that may cause asthma.

The Digestive System

This is what the human digestive system looks like:

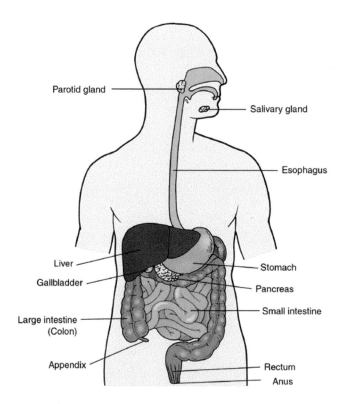

Outline of the human digestive system

You only need to learn these bits: oesophagus, stomach, small intestine, large intestine, rectum; as well as the glands associated with the digestive system: the salivary glands and the pancreas.

Put simply, the definition of digestion is:

Digestion is the process in which large molecules are hydrolysed by enzymes to produce smaller molecules that can be absorbed and assimilated.

into the blood stream.

It starts in the mouth where food is moistened by saliva and broken down into small parts by chewing. The resulting "bolus" of food is swallowed and travels down the oesophagus and into the stomach, where stomach acid breaks the food down further by breaking the chemical bonds in it. By the time it's reached the small intestine, food particles are small enough to be absorbed. The leftovers pass down into the large intestine, and then leave the system by a process well known as pooping.

Proteins

Proteins are at the heart of living organisms. Their functions are very varied, from the hair on your head, to the haemoglobin in your red blood cells (which carries oxygen around the body), to the claws of a lion, to insulin (blood glucose regulation). All these highly varied proteins are made of their building blocks - amino acids. This is what the generalised structure of an amino acid looks like (make sure you can draw this):

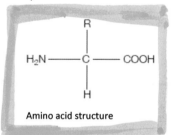

Amino acid structure

If you're wondering what this actually is, read on. The clues are in the name (as they usually are).

AMINO - the NH_2 on the left hand side is an amino group

ACID - the COOH on the right hand side is a carboxylic acid group (simply an acid)

The hydrogen (H) on the bottom is there all the time (just like the amino group and the acid group), while the R group is the variable which determines what particular amino acid this will be. For example, if the R group were a hydrogen, the amino acid would be glycine.

The next diagram shows condensation, and the subsequent formation of a bond between two amino acids (any two). This bond is a peptide bond. The resulting molecule is called a polypeptide.

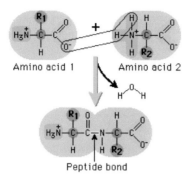

Two amino acids are joined by a peptide bond

The theme of protein structure versus function is really strongly played on in exams, throughout A level biology. The core idea must be learnt, and this is it:

Proteins have a primary, secondary, tertiary and (some only) quaternary structure. The tertiary structure of proteins is their 3D shape which is highly folded and has a unique structure. This structure gives proteins their specific function. For example, if insulin were misfolded, it would cease to function properly. Of course though, the origin of misfolding is likely to be in the primary structure, due to a mutation.

Enzyme Action

Enzymes are proteins which catalyse (speed up) metabolic reactions. Like all other catalysts (e.g. in chemistry), enzymes achieve this by lowering the activation energy (energy needed for a reaction to occur) of a reaction, by forming an enzyme-substrate complex.

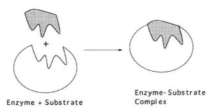

Formation of the enzyme-substrate complex

This can be described by the lock and key, and induced fit models of enzyme action. The lock and key model is based on complementary shapes between the enzyme and substrate. The substrate fits into the enzyme.

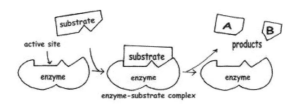

Enzymes catalyse substrate reactions (State of New South Wales)

The induced fit model (the enzyme changes shape to "hug" the substrate):

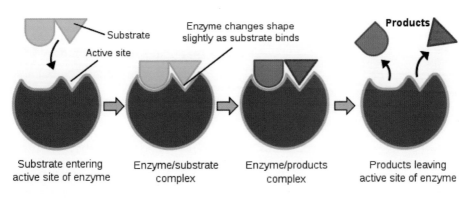

Induced fit model

The enzyme shape is not exactly matched to the substrate, but it is able to accommodate the substrate with a close enough shape into an enzyme-substrate complex and carry out catalysing that reaction.

Enzyme Properties

Enzymes are crucial to proper metabolic function, and ultimately life. That is why you need to know the conditions which affect enzyme activity. There are several properties which can alter enzyme function:

1. Temperature

2. Inhibitors (competitive and non-competitive)

3. pH

4. Substrate concentration

An enzyme is a protein, so has a delicate tertiary structure that enables adequate function. High temperature or pH would alter its tertiary structure. Inhibitors would bind to its active site, preventing substrates from doing so. This results in no enzyme-substrate complexe being formed. Let's have a closer look at these properties individually.

Temperature

Increasing temperature results in a higher rate of activity, up to a certain point where the enzyme becomes denatured. A high temperature causes the molecule to vibrate, breaking the weak bonds that hold it together, and changing the structure of the enzyme. This process is denaturation. The point at which this happens is usually around 50 - 60 degrees Celsius.

Denatured enzymes don't work. Look at this graph to understand the relationship between enzyme activity and temperature:

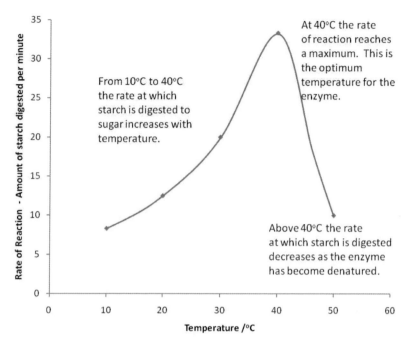

From 10°C to 40°C the rate at which starch is digested to sugar increases with temperature.

At 40°C the rate of reaction reaches a maximum. This is the optimum temperature for the enzyme.

Above 40°C the rate at which starch is digested decreases as the enzyme has become denatured.

Effect of temperature on enzyme activity

Inhibitors

Inhibitors are molecules which interfere with the substrate binding to the active site of an enzyme, slowing down or stopping the reaction. These may be reversible or non-reversible inhibitors. The reversible inhibitors can be competitive or non-competitive.

Competitive inhibitors have a similar 3D shape to the substrate, hence they can bind to the active site of the enzyme, preventing the substrate from doing so. It's easy to picture:

Competitive inhibitors bind at the substrate site

The competitive inhibitor competes (as you'd expect) with the substrate for the active site of the enzyme. If more substrate is added, then the inhibitor's effect will be diminished. This is what the graph looks like (make sure you can recall this):

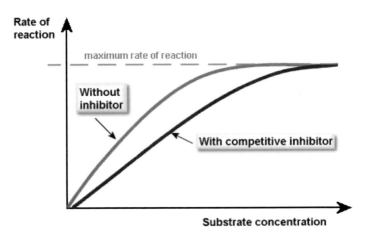

Effect of competitive inhibitor on rate of reaction

Non-competitive inhibitors on the other hand bind to the enzyme at a site away from the active site. All good? No, because that results in the enzyme changing shape. This means the substrate can no longer bind to the active site. Unlike the case of competitive inhibitors, changing the substrate concentration will not have an effect on the rate of reaction. Here is a comparison diagram and a comparison graph (learn these):

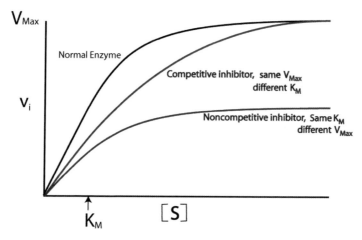

The effect of competitive and non-competitive inhibitors on reaction rate with increasing substrate concentration

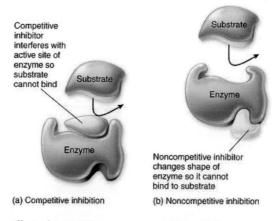

Effects of competitive and non-competitive inhibitors

Don't worry about the V (velocity), check your textbook for other graphs.

pH

Binding of the substrate to the enzyme depends on a close match between shape and charge. The pH is a measure of the concentration of H^+ ions versus OH^- ions. As you can see, these are positively or negatively charged, so a really high or really low pH can disrupt enzyme function. All enzymes have a specific optimal pH at which they work best. This differs between enzymes. For example, while most enzymes work best at a pH of 7.35 (that is halfway between 1 and 14 where 1 is most acidic and 14 is most basic), pepsin in the stomach acid works best at a pH of 3.

Substrate concentration

This topic is a matter of common sense. However, you must use A level language. Here it goes.

Common sense version: More substrate results in more reactions, so rate of reaction goes up. Of course, when all enzymes are working all the time, adding even more substrate will not increase the rate of reaction, unless more enzyme is added.

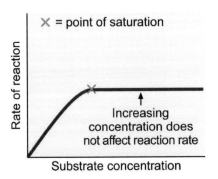

Effect of substrate concentration on reaction rate

A level language version: The higher the substrate concentration, the faster the rate of reaction until the enzymes are working as fast as possible. This is when all the active sites are filled all the time. From this point, the only way to increase the rate any further is to add more enzyme.

Final tip: on this topic, the specification emphasises that you should be aware of the lock and key versus induced fit models. The induced fit model is better because it suggests the enzyme changes shape slightly to accommodate the shape of the substrate. This is beneficial if the enzyme is perhaps fluctuating in shape due to changes in temperature for example.

Carbohydrate Digestion

Carbohydrates as well as proteins are polymers and contain only a few different types of atom. In the case of carbohydrates, the basic molecular units are called monosaccharides - these are the monomers. (Mono = single; poly = multiple; saccharide = sugar)

α (alpha) glucose is the most important monosaccharide to learn, as you need to be able to draw it:

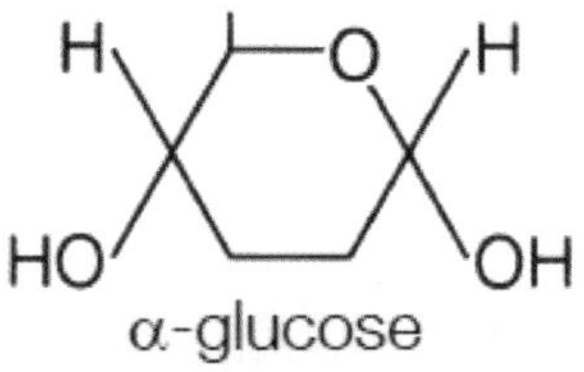

α-glucose

Structure of α glucose

The points where the lines intersect each symbolise a carbon (C) atom. You need not show those. The figure above is taken from the specification itself, so take it as a good guide. The monosaccharide alpha glucose (commonly, just glucose) somehow becomes a polysaccharide. This is achieved by condensation reactions, and the bonds formed are called glycosidic bonds.

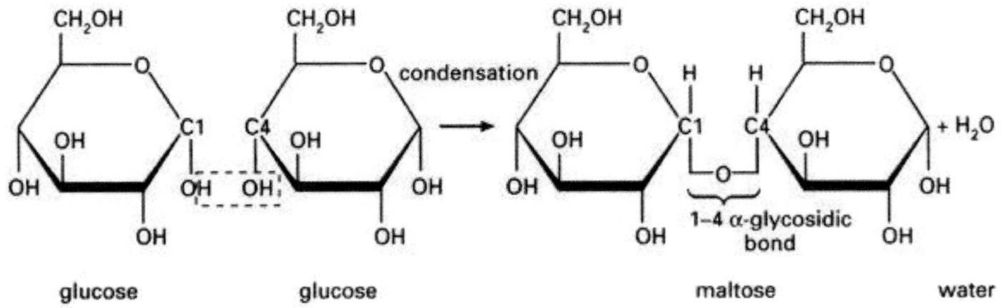

Condensation reaction between two glucose monomers forms maltose

You should be able to draw this. The resulting molecule, maltose, is a disaccharide (two monomers). If you keep adding glucose molecules to the chain, you get... *drum roll please* ...starch. Starch is made up of multiple (very many indeed) monomers, so it is a polymer i.e. it is made of multiple monosaccharides, so it is a polysaccharide.

Potatoes anyone?

You also need to know about two other disaccharides and their constituent monosaccharides - sucrose and lactose.

Sucrose is made of glucose and fructose.

Lactose is made of glucose and galactose.

It's easy enough to remember: they're both made of glucose, and lactose (MILK) is also made of galactose (galaxy - Milky Way). Both sucrose and lactose are formed similarly by the condensation of their monosaccharides.

During digestion, these large molecules must be broken back down into small molecules. Starch must be broken down to glucose. Enzymes produced by the salivary glands and the pancreas carry out this reaction in the mouth and stomach. One particular such enzyme is amylase. By the time food reaches the small intestine where nutrients are absorbed, glucose on its own must be made available for absorption in the epithelial cells lining the intestine. This is achieved by maltase, which breaks down... that's right, maltose, leaving behind single molecules of glucose.

Regarding lactose you need to be aware of lactose intolerance. Just as for starch or maltose, lactose too must be broken down successfully for its monomers (glucose and galactose) to be absorbed by the body. Not surprisingly, this is achieved by the enzyme lactase. People deficient of this enzyme will not properly digest, or break down lactose from milk, so lactose will go unchecked into the large intestine, where microorganisms will use it for respiration, leaving behind a lot of gas. This causes symptoms like bloating, abdominal pain and diarrhoea.

Sugars can be reducing or non-reducing, depending on their chemistry (you do not want to go into that. Unless you're into chemistry). All monosaccharides, and the disaccharides lactose and maltose are reducing sugars. All else including sucrose is non-reducing. Benedict's reagent is a test for reducing and non-reducing sugars.

Benedict's reagent = light blue

You throw some glucose into the mix = orange/brick red due to it being reducing (reduces copper ions Cu^{2+} to Cu^+)

You become adventurous and throw some sucrose into the mix = ends it utter disappointment when you get nothing, light blue, due to it not being reducing.

And finally, there is a test for starch. Chop a potato (they are practically made of the stuff) and add iodine which is yellow. The starch in the potato will turn it blue. This is a very simple test for starch - if the solution stays yellow it's negative, if it goes blue, it's positive.

Cells

Specifically, this topic is about the epithelial cells lining the small intestine. These cells are animal cells, and their function is to absorb nutrients as part of digestion. This is what epithelial cells look like under a light microscope:

Epithelial cells of the small intestine

The core components of cells are the outer membrane, the cytoplasm (substance inside which contains all other stuff) and the nucleus (contains DNA). All the other stuff is made up of various components with specific functions - these are called organelles. The ones you must know about are:

1. Plasma membrane, including cell-surface membrane

2. Microvilli

3. Nucleus

4. Mitochondria

5. Lysosomes

6. Ribosomes

7. Endoplasmic reticulum

8. Golgi apparatus

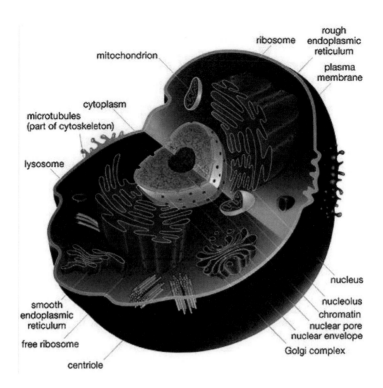

Outline of animal cell (Mountain Empire Community College)

A bit about each...

Plasma membrane = thin boundary between cell and environment

It is made of a phospholipid bilayer, and its function is to control what passes through the cell. Membranes are also found in other organelles such as the nucleus and mitochondria.

Phospholipid bilayer

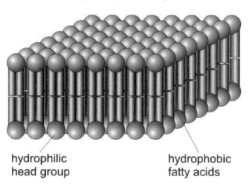

hydrophilic head group

hydrophobic fatty acids

Two layers of phospholipids

Nucleus

Usually it is the large rounded organelle in a cell. It has a double membrane with many pores through which materials can pass. Each cell normally has one nucleus. The main functions are cell division, replication and protein synthesis.

Mitochondrion (mitochondria, plural)

This is basically the easily identifiable sausage-like organelle with the cool inner membrane that forms the cristae. It is the site of aerobic respiration, where most ATP is made. Look:

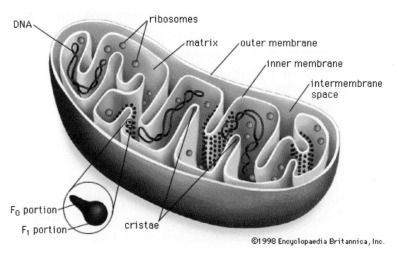

DNA
ribosomes
matrix
outer membrane
inner membrane
intermembrane space
F_0 portion
F_1 portion
cristae

©1998 Encyclopaedia Britannica, Inc.

Outline of mitochondrion structure (Encyclopaedia Britannica)

Endoplasmic reticulum

There are two different kinds of endoplasmic reticulum - rough and smooth endoplasmic reticulum, hence their short names rough ER and smooth ER. The roughness and smoothness business is down to ribosomes attached to the rough ER, but not to smooth ER.

Rough ER - transport system: collects, stores, packages and transports the proteins made on the ribosomes

Smooth ER - synthesis of lipids and some steroids; detoxification e.g. alcohol breakdown.

What does it look like??? Well, imagine this is a bit like the inner membrane of the mitochondria, but more tightly packed.

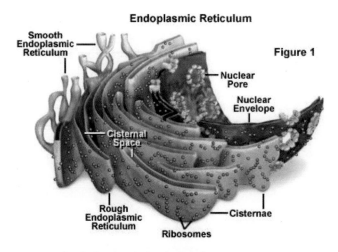

Structure of endoplasmic reticulum in the cell

Microvilli

Microvilli are really just protrusions of the plasma membrane. They're like fingers coming out of a hand. The reason they are so relevant to epithelial cells lining the small intestine is that microvilli increase the surface area onto which nutrients can be absorbed. This is a key concept.

Lysosomes

These are small vesicles of membrane that contain enzymes which take part in digestion. They look like tiny balls.

Ribosomes

My personal favourite :) Ribosomes are made of a small subunit and a large subunit. They are found on the rough ER and free within the cytoplasm, and they are the site of translation where the genetic code is used to build protein. Under the microscope within a cell, they appear as mere dots. But remember, awesome comes in small quantities!

Golgi apparatus

It is a stack of flattened membrane discs which receives packages of protein from the rough ER, and is also involved in synthesising chemicals before they are secreted from the cell.

Microscopes

You will need to know about the difference between transmission and scanning electron microscopes – TEM and SEM. Both (as the name suggests) use a beam of electrons, rather than light, to produce an image of the sample. TEM uses electrons which pass through the sample, so the resulting micrograph (image) shows everything within the sample in black and white, for example organelles in a cell. SEM uses electrons which scan the sample in 3D, resulting in a coloured micrograph with 3D detail, but no components from within the sample.

SEM of human flea head (Steve Gschmeissner) and TEM of cell components

When talking about microscopes, differentiating between resolution and magnification is important. In principle, it's not hard to understand. Imagine zooming in a photo to try to see a detail. That is magnification. Now imagine the photo has a low resolution, and if you magnify it, you can only see annoying pixels. If the image had a high resolution, you would be able to see the detail clearly after zooming in. So magnifying is zooming in, while resolution is the focus power. You will need to be able to calculate actual sizes and magnifications of various drawings. The equation for that is:

Image size on paper = magnification x actual size

The theory is all good, but in practice, someone's gotta mash those cells, separate organelles and what not. The technique used is called cell fractionation and it involves ultracentrifugation. These are the steps:

1. Take some tissue such as liver, and blend it in a blender; this is called homogenisation. This must be done in a special solution – an isotonic buffer. Isotonic means of the same water potential as the sample. This ensures enzyme reactions are minimised, organelles don't get distorted by water gain or loss, and changes in pH are resisted. Learn this (examiners have the hots for isotonic buffers).

2. The resulting mixture is filtered to remove any debris, and then spun in an ultracentrifuge very fast. The increased gravitational field produced will separate the organelles according to their density and even shape.

3. The big ol' nuclei are the first to separate. The other organelles, still in the liquid at the top called supernatant, are poured into a different test tube and centrifuged further.

4. The organelles are separated in the order: mitochondria and lysosomes, rough ER, plasma membranes, smooth ER, ribosomes.

Plasma Membranes

Membranes are made of phospholipids, which are made of lipids. Lipids are the stuff of oils, fats and waxes. Unlike proteins and carbohydrates, lipids are not polymers. Lipids which store energy are triglycerides, while those which form membranes are phospholipids. Triglycerides are formed by a molecule of glycerol with three fatty acids attached. The reaction which results in triglycerides is condensation.

Three fatty acids are bound to one glycerol molecule

Glycerol (green) + 3x fatty acids (red)

The fatty acids can be simplified in drawing:

$$
\begin{array}{c}
\text{O} \quad\ \text{H} \\
\| \quad\quad\ | \\
\text{C-O-C-H} \\
\text{O} \quad\quad\ | \\
\| \quad\quad\ | \\
\text{C-O-C-H} \\
\text{O} \quad\quad\ | \\
\| \quad\quad\ | \\
\text{C-O-C-H} \\
\text{H}
\end{array}
$$

3 Fatty Acids + Glycerol

Triglyceride structure

The bonds formed (C-O) are called ester bonds. Fatty acids can be saturated or unsaturated (monounsaturated; polyunsaturated). Saturated fatty acids have all their carbon (C) atoms linked to hydrogen (H) atoms, hence saturated with hydrogen. If there is a carbon atom with a double bond to its neighbour carbon atom, then it will only have one bond to a hydrogen atom, hence it is unsaturated.

If there is one double bond present, the fatty acid is monounsaturated. If there are multiple double bonds present, the fatty acid is polyunsaturated.

In phospholipids one of the fatty acids is replaced by a phosphate group.

Phospholipid

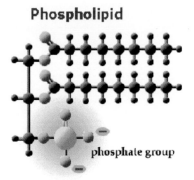

phosphate group

Phospholipid structure (Professor John Blamire)

The test for lipids is the emulsion test. This test takes advantage of the ability of lipids to dissolve in ethanol (alcohol), but not in water. You dissolve the sample into ethanol by shaking, then pour it into water. If milky white droplets are formed, the sample is positive for lipids.

Armed with this knowledge of lipids, as well as carbohydrates and proteins, we can now explore the structure of plasma membranes, specifically in the context of the fluid-mosaic model. Phospholipids have a hydrophilic (water loving) head, and hydrophobic (water repelling) tails. This results in the formation of a phospholipid bilayer (double layer), which forms the basis for the plasma membrane.

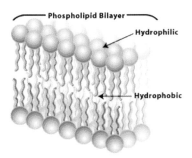

Phospholipid bilayer

The name of fluid-mosaic model comes from:

Fluid = the arrangement of proteins contained in the membrane is always changing

Mosaic = the proteins present are spread around in a mosaic-like fashion.

Plasma Membrane Structural Components

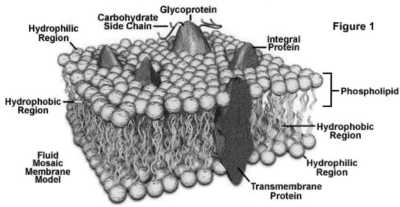

Elements in a plasma membrane (Michael W. Davidson)

It's pretty isn't it? The proteins are crucial to cell communication as well as the selective permeability of the membrane. The glycoprotein (sugars/carbohydrates attached to a protein) side chains act as receptors. Lipid soluble stuff such as vitamins A, D and K, as well as oxygen and carbon dioxide, can pass freely though the membrane.

The specification emphasises the importance of understanding the role of microvilli. These are elongations of plasma membrane which increase the surface area available for reaction or absorption.

Diffusion

Diffusion = the spread of particles from a region of higher concentration to a region of lower concentration, until the particles are evenly spread out.

Diffusion takes place when you use a spray in a room, for example. The particles in the spray move randomly, knocking each other, which results in them spreading throughout the room gradually, from high concentration to low concentration. Therefore, diffusion acts down (or along) a concentration gradient.

It is important to know what factors affect the rate of diffusion. These are:

1. Surface area - the greater the surface area, the faster diffusion will occur

2. Difference in concentration - the higher the difference (the steeper the gradient), the faster diffusion will take place

3. The thickness of the exchange surface - the thicker the exchange surface, the slower the rate of diffusion

Of course there are other factors such as temperature (increased kinetic energy results in faster diffusion) and the diffusion pathway (distance). The latter is a side effect of (3.) The thickness of the exchange surface, in some respects.

In some cases, diffusion is aided by certain proteins. This is called facilitated diffusion. The responsible proteins speed up diffusion of substances which would otherwise take longer to pass through the plasma membrane.

The key points about facilitated diffusion which differentiate it from active transport (which also uses proteins):

-it occurs down a concentration gradient

-it uses no metabolic energy

Two kinds of protein achieve facilitated diffusion: carrier proteins and ion channels. Carrier proteins transport substances from one side of the membrane to the other, usually by co-transport. For example, glucose is transported along with a Na^+ ion.

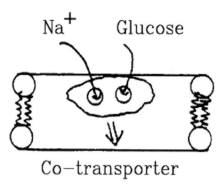

Co-transport of glucose and sodium ions

Ion channels are proteins with gates that can be opened or closed to allow or stop certain ions from entering, e.g. Na⁺ (sodium) and K⁺ (potassium) ions.

Osmosis

Osmosis is the diffusion of water across a semi-permeable membrane. The "concentration" of water is referred to as water potential. So osmosis is the movement of water from a higher water potential to a lower water potential across a membrane.

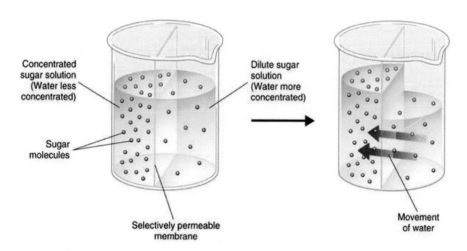

Osmosis experiment

For osmosis to occur it is essential that there is a semi-permeable membrane separating two environments with a different solute concentration. The solute must be unable to cross the membrane (molecules too big), but the water molecules are free to pass through and lead to an equilibrium. In the previous image, the right side of the beaker has a higher water potential than the left side, so water moves in from right to left.

You must also learn the term isotonic. A solution is isotonic when it has the same water potential as another solution. An example is Ringer's solution which has the same water potential as blood plasma, so can be used to keep tissues alive.

Active Transport

Unlike diffusion, osmosis and facilitated diffusion, active transport requires energy in the form of ATP (adenosine triphosphate), and moves substances against a concentration gradient (from a lower concentration to a higher concentration). This process is essential in removing all toxins from the body, as well as the movement of rare chemicals.

Active transport is achieved by specific carrier proteins in the plasma membrane, and relies on adequate oxygen supply (which results in ATP being available).

There are certain cells which carry out active transport more than others, for example in the kidney. These cells have special adaptations, such as microvilli for increased surface area, hence more carrier proteins available, as well as many mitochondria for the production of ATP.

Absorption

When carbohydrates from food are digested, lots of glucose molecules, along with some fructose and galactose, are produced in the small intestine. Initially the mode of transport of glucose in absorption is diffusion. It is then followed by facilitated diffusion via co-transport, where glucose molecules are absorbed along with a sodium ion (Na^+) through a carrier protein. This method is much faster than diffusion by itself.

Both Na^+ and glucose must be present for absorption by co-transport to take place.

That's it, be glad this is a small topic :)

Cholera

Cholera is an infectious disease caused by *Vibrio cholerae*, which is a major cause of death in areas of the world where a proper infrastructure for good sanitation doesn't exist. Bacteria are ingested by consuming contaminated water and food. The water becomes contaminated when a person with the disease (which causes severe diarrhoea) produces the faeces which then carry the bacteria in the water supply.

As all bacteria, *Vibrio cholerae* is a prokaryotic organism. Prokaryotes do not have a nucleus like eukaryotes do. Their DNA is not membrane-bound, just free in the cytoplasm.

Prokaryotic Cell Structure

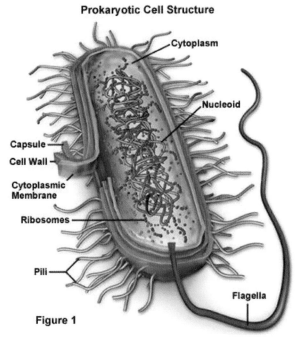

Figure 1

Overview of a prokaryotic cell

The features of prokaryotic cells you must learn are:

-Cell wall

-Cell-surface membrane

-Capsule (protective layer)

-Circular DNA (as all DNA, it stores the genetic information)

-Flagella (used for movement – think sperm cells)

-Plasmid (small loop of DNA which can be copied and passed on to other bacteria by conjugation)

The cholera bacteria cause severe diarrhoea by producing a toxin which binds to receptors in the small intestine; this in turn activates cyclic AMP (which is a messenger molecule) which results in chloride pumps staying open all the time. Under normal conditions, these pumps would open and close accordingly to adjust water content in the small intestine. In cholera however, chloride ions are free to rush out into the lumen ("empty" space), as well as other ions such as sodium. This causes the water potential in the lumen to decrease (so water moves in by osmosis from cells lining the small intestine into the lumen), which results in a high amount of water being lost from the body.

All is not lost though, because the treatment for cholera is indeed easily available and relatively cheap. This is called oral rehydration therapy with Oral Rehydration Solutions (ORS). When the body loses many essential ions and water by severe diarrhoea, the solution (pun intended) is an oral rehydration solution which throws much needed water and nutrients e.g. glucose (for energy), calcium, chloride, sodium and potassium, back into the patient.

ORS = 1 L water + 8 teaspoonfuls sugar + 1 teaspoonful salt

This is a basic DIY recipe, but pharmaceutical companies work on better recipes.

You should be aware of the ethical aspects of using ORS when there are experimental trials on humans. They must do it voluntarily, consent to it, have it carried out by professionals, and have the risks associated with the trial minimised. On the other hand, lives must be saved even though children may not be able to consent, and poor countries may not have trained professionals to carry out the trials. It's all about balance.

Lung Function

The human gas exchange system is made of the trachea, from which the bronchi branch off, followed by the bronchioles into the lungs, and finally the alveoli, which are the functional unit of the lungs. Of course this is nonsense without an image:

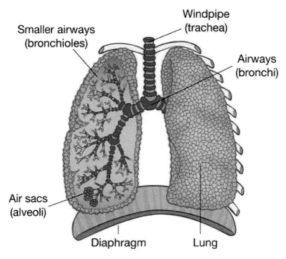

Respiratory system components

Air enters the lungs via the trachea, bronchi and bronchioles into the tiny air sacs - the alveoli. The epithelium of the alveoli is extremely thin (just one-cell wide, in fact) to allow fast diffusion of oxygen into the red blood cells, and of carbon dioxide out of them. The capillaries surrounding alveoli are so narrow, that the red blood cells have to be squished in order to pass through. This shortens the diffusion pathway, which in turn increases the rate of diffusion.

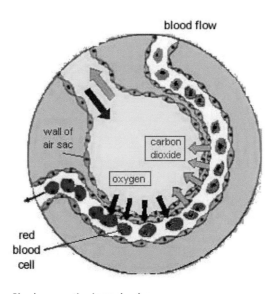

Blood oxygenation in an alveolus

What allows diffusion to take place, of course, is the concentration gradient formed between the air in the alveoli and the red blood cells. Red blood cells deprived of oxygen and loaded with carbon dioxide (the blue/purple ones) will release carbon dioxide into the fresh air, then take up oxygen from it afterwards.

Since lungs aren't made of muscle, how is their movement brought about in ventilation (breathing)? Intercostal (between-ribs) muscles and the diaphragm are responsible. Their contraction is caused by nerve signals from the respiratory centre in the medulla (in the brain). This results in the intercostal muscles pulling the ribs up, while the diaphragm is flat, and the abdominal organs are pushed downwards. The thorax (chest cavity) increases in volume, so lowers its pressure below that of the atmosphere, resulting in air being drawn into the lungs. Exhaling, on the other hand, does not require muscular activity. Elastic recoil of the muscles, as well as the weight of the ribcage and abdominal organs, result in the pressure inside the lungs increasing, therefore pushing the air back outside.

In medicine, it's important to have a calculation for the amount of air a person takes in or out over time.

Pulmonary ventilation = tidal volume x ventilation rate

Tidal volume is the volume of air inhaled or exhaled in one breath.

Ventilation rate is the number of breaths taken in one minute.

So, if someone were breathing 20 times a minute a volume of 300 cm^3 per breath, what would their pulmonary ventilation be?

By the above formula, 300 cm^3 x 20 = 6000 cm^3. Simplified, this is 6 litres per minute.

The Biological Basis of Lung Disease

Tuberculosis (TB) is an infectious disease of the lungs which causes constant coughing with blood, shortness of breath, fever and weight loss over the years. Every year two million people die from TB out of 8/10 million who get the disease. Far more people, around two billion, carry the TB bacteria on them without having the disease.

TB is passed on between people by inhaling droplets from the air infected with the bacteria *Mycobacterium tuberculosis*. When the infection is confirmed, patients are isolated for up to four weeks and put on a course of antibiotics for up to 6 months.

When bacteria reach the alveoli, the immune system reacts by surrounding them with white blood cells, which results in the formation of scar tissue.

The shortness of breath symptom is caused by less oxygen reaching the circulatory system due to a decreased surface area for diffusion in the lungs, as many alveoli are damaged.

TB is the main disease covered, and there are three additional lung diseases you should know about. These are:

1. Fibrosis

2. Emphysema

3. Asthma

Fibrosis

Fibrosis is the accumulation of scar tissue as a result of damage or bacterial infection. It affects the alveoli primarily, as they are ever so small and fragile.

This occurs in smokers, due to air pollution, or indeed in TB. So fibrosis is not a disease in its own right, but a result of others.

Scar tissue is fibrous connective tissue and prevents good lung function, therefore symptoms caused are coughing and shortness of breath. Damaged alveoli will not contribute to the diffusion of oxygen into red blood cells.

Emphysema

Emphysema is a nasty disease. It is caused by excessive smoking (or air pollutants) over a lifetime and results in a steep decline in lung function, to the point where very severe cases require an oxygen tank connected to the airways at all times.

Fibrosis occurs in the lungs, which results in thicker alveolar walls which increase the diffusion pathway of oxygen and carbon dioxide, therefore decreasing the rate of diffusion. Another side effect is a loss of elasticity which makes breathing out more difficult.

Asthma

Asthma does not incur any damage to the lungs like the previous diseases do. Fibrosis does not take place, and the surface area of the alveoli is unaffected. What does take place is that the terminal bronchiole smooth muscles constrict, resulting in less air reaching the lungs. Symptoms include short-term shortness of breath and an increased secretion of mucus.

Things which bring on asthma (which is an exaggerated, unnecessary immune response) include stress, cold, exercise and air pollution. It is treated with antihistamines and steroids, which reduce the response, as well as bronchodilators which relax the smooth muscles.

Heart Structure and Function

In my quest to find a suitable diagram for the heart, this is what I found:

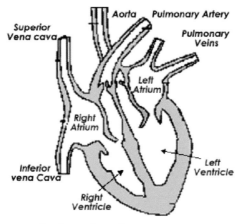

Heart chambers and vessels

Definitely use your textbook as a guide on this. It only takes a google search to realise the ridiculous number of variations of diagrams for the heart and different annotations.

You need to be able to sketch a heart and label the main veins, valves, arteries and aorta, and the ventricles and atria.

There are two types of circulation going on via the heart: pulmonary circulation and systemic circulation. Pulmonary circulation is a short-distance route between the heart and the lungs, where deoxygenated blood is taken to be replenished with oxygen. Although normally veins take blood away, and arteries take blood to, in the case of pulmonary circulation things are the opposite way around. The pulmonary vein brings freshly oxygenated blood into the heart (left atrium), while the pulmonary artery takes deoxygenated blood back from the right ventricle into the lungs.

The atrioventricular valves and semilunar valves play an important role in ensuring proper heart function. The former ensure no blood flows back into the atria from the ventricles, while the latter ensure no blood flows from the ventricles into the atria.

Electrical impulses cause heart muscle contraction which creates an increased pressure of blood, resulting in it being pushed in a certain direction, with the valves opening in its way. The sequence of events in heart contraction is this:

1. Both atria contract - atrial systole

2. Both ventricles contract - ventricular systole

3. All chambers relax – diastole

The heart muscle contracts without brain stimulation - the brain only controls the speed. Electrical impulses start in the sino-atrial node in the right atrium, travel down to the atrio-ventricular node, which then spreads it across the bundle of His, which results in the left ventricle contracting.

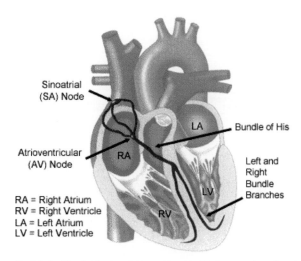

Electrical wiring in the heart (Texas Heart Institute, www.texasheart.org)

Cardiac output = heart rate x stroke volume

Heart rate is measured in beats per minute, while stroke volume is measured in cm^3 or ml.

Make sure you can interpret graphs showing the sequence of atria and ventricles contracting followed by diastole.

The Biological Basis of Heart Disease

Atheroma, aneurysm, thrombosis, myocardial infarction?

Read on to learn what these words mean. Coronary heart disease is a major cause of death in the UK and much of the rest of the world.

Risk factors associated with CHD are diet, blood cholesterol, cigarette smoking and high blood pressure.

Atheroma

This is the build-up of fatty material in the walls of arteries. It is often the underlying cause that leads to heart disease.

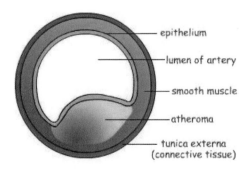

Atheroma in the artery

As you can see, it leads to the narrowing of arteries, causing a lowering of blood supply. Atheroma is associated with an increased risk of aneurysm and thrombosis. Aneurysm is a ballooning of the artery which weakens the affected area. This requires urgent treatment, otherwise it is fatal if the balloon "pops". Thrombosis is a blood clot stuck in a vessel which results in less blood supply to a specific area, and the subsequent affected tissues may be starved of blood and die.

If the blood supply to the heart muscle is stopped, then a myocardial infarction occurs. This is the scientific name for a heart attack. The heart muscle (or part of it) dies as a result of a lack of oxygen from the blood.

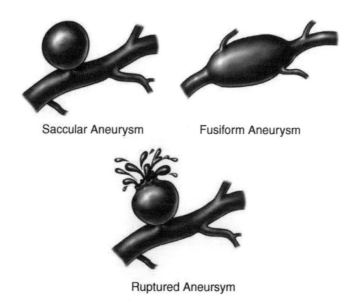

Saccular Aneurysm   Fusiform Aneurysm

Ruptured Aneursym

Types of aneurysm

These are different kinds of aneurysm (you don't need to learn the names).

Diet

Stuff like sugary food and processed meat contain high levels of simple sugars and cholesterol respectively which can lead up to atheroma. Plants on the other hand have little cholesterol, so by far the easiest way to cut on cholesterol is to remove meat from the diet, especially fatty meats. Cholesterol levels are also genetically inherited, in which case diet is even more important in preventing CHD. There are two kinds of cholesterol, HDL and LDL. HDL has a positive impact on health by removing blood cholesterol and sending it to the liver; LDL has a negative impact by doing the exact opposite - carrying cholesterol from the liver to other cells in the body.

Smoking

The mechanism by which smoking causes CHD (specifically arthrosclerosis = hardening of the arteries) is complex and not fully mapped out yet. However, it is known that certain substances contained in tobacco lead to artery constriction, which in turn raises blood pressure.

Principles of Immunology

Immunity against invading pathogens is a crucial part of maintaining health. The body has adaptations which prevent invasion by pathogens, as well as processes in place to deal with those that manage to penetrate the body's primary defences. The skin and mucous membranes (e.g. mouth) are examples of such defences. Sweat contains lysozyme which is an enzyme that breaks down bacterial walls.

If pathogens do invade the body, the subsequent immune response is split between:

1. Non-specific

2. Specific

The non-specific immune response is inflammation and phagocytosis.

Phagocytosis

White cells (the most common ones are neutrophils) engulf any foreign particle such as dust or bacteria, then digest it and dispose of the remains. It's badass, trust me.

The enzymes used to break invaders down are in lysosomes which fuse with the vesicle which contains the bacteria. All this action happens within the white cell. At the end, the undigested leftovers are disposed of by exocytosis (kind of like a burp).

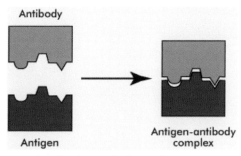

Formation of antigen-antibody complex

Antibodies are made by B cells or T cells which come from stem cells from bone marrow. B cells release antibodies, while T cells secrete antibodies which stay on the surface of the cell.

B cell → O -- - - - -

T cell → O-

Where "-" is an antibody. Apologies for the horrendous visual representation.

So when a bacterium invades, B cells release antibodies with a shape complementary to that of the bacterium's antigen. This antibody then binds to the antigen. T cells on the other hand secrete the antibodies on their surface, then personally greet the bacterium and bind to it via the antibody. You could say the B cell is shooting the bacterium, while the T cell is strangling it. But for goodness' sake, don't write that in the exam.

When a pathogen invades the body and a B cell releases the appropriate antibody to manage the infection, it's not just the one B cell. They come in their thousands, they are clones of a B cell with a specific antibody, and they are called plasma cells. Plasma cells release a high amount of antibodies, but they are short-lived. Other cells called memory cells may survive for much longer, up to several years.

Memory cells are involved in the secondary immune response which happens if a high enough amount of antigens are present. The memory cells replicate into a large number of plasma cells which then release enough antibodies.

Common flu

OK, so if we have all these fancy cells doing our work for us, how come the cold virus gets us again and again and again? Surely our memory cells could identify the cold virus, replicate and defeat it?

Memory cells are specific to certain antigens. The flu virus has many different variations of antigens which change constantly, so by the time we've acquired some resistance to this year's antigen, a new one will have emerged.

Vaccinations

Vaccinations prevent symptoms of an illness (such as flu) from developing, by creating a primary immune response to a harmless substance that the body identifies as a pathogen. This could be an antigen, or the pathogen itself - dead or otherwise modified to prevent disease. Some vaccines are really successful and have prevented many diseases so far, yet the flu vaccine remains a challenge due to the above points. The virus changes its antigens, and there is great variation to start off with.

Monoclonal antibodies

These are antibodies which can be cloned from a single cell to make a high amount of them. They can bind to pretty much any substance, and are used in pregnancy tests as well as cancer treatment. The process involves taking a cell which produces antibodies such as a lymphocyte, and crossing it with a tumour cell. Tumour cells divide uncontrollably, so the end hybrid cell will produce many antibodies via its many clones.

How Science Works

You need to be able to evaluate data regarding the use of vaccines and monoclonal antibodies, as well as discuss the ethical issues arising from the testing and use of vaccines.

Part II

Investigating Variation

Variation between members of the same species is called intraspecific variation. Members of different species are easily distinguishable as very different (interspecific variation), but variation is a key concept within the same species too. So if you were to collect samples of clovers in order to analyse their height, how would you go about making sure you don't happen to pick up all the tall ones or all the short ones? Before you've even analysed them, how would you know what the average height would be?

Chance plays an important role in sampling. Chance cannot be eliminated, but the probability of variation being due to chance can be decreased by collecting a large sample, and random sampling. In this case, the height of clovers would be considered continuous variation, as opposed to discontinuous. Continuous means that the clovers can have any height between certain values e.g. 2.1 cm, 2.2 cm or 2.25 cm. Could one clover have a height of 2.24 cm? Yes, that's perfectly possible.

An example of discontinuous variation is the number of toes. It's either 10, or more rarely a couple more or a couple less. So it could be 8, 10 or 12. Could someone have 12.35 toes? No.

Back to the clovers. You've got the data, and if you were to plot it, then what you'd get is a normal distribution curve. This means that most clovers will have about the same height, with a few deviating from the mean. The extent to which deviation from the mean occurs is called the standard deviation. This shows the spread of data around the mean.

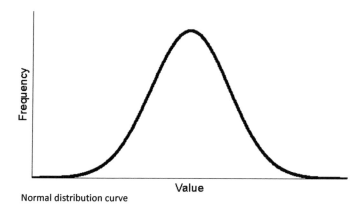

Normal distribution curve

The middle value, which is the mean, will have the highest frequency, whereas the extreme values i.e. midget clovers and gigantoclovers will have the lowest frequency.

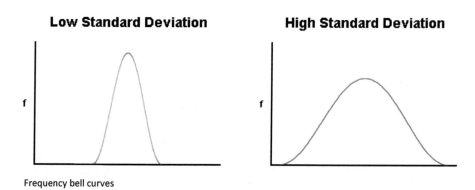

Frequency bell curves

The first graph would show a sample of clovers where the vast majority have a similar height, and only a few deviate from the mean. The second graph would represent the heights of a clover sample where most have a similar height, and a significant number deviate from the mean.

Causes of Variation

Variation is central to life itself. Variation is what makes every single individual... an individual. Without variation, the evolution of different species would not be possible. What is the cause of variation?

Genes

Genes dictate what proteins our body makes, when, where and how, and are ultimately responsible for the way we look and function. It's not just what genes we have though, it's also about whether they are switched on or off, when they are switched on or off, and in which particular cells they are switched on or off. Us and chimps share a great deal of our genotype (genetic makeup), more than 98%, yet we can agree that there are significant differences between us that make us distinct species.

Features such as height, predisposition to illness, weight, or even behaviours such as risk-taking have been linked exclusively or partly to certain genes.

Environment

The environment is not just what most people associate with the word. It's not just the temperature of the room you live in - it's everything outside (and inside) our bodies which exert their influence on it. Which is pretty much everything from family and friends, to the internet and diet, exercise, culture and beyond. The environment in the womb where we grew had an impact on our bodies. Even the environment of genes themselves has an impact on their activity.

Genes won't result in the variation seen in a professional body building contest. Those physiques were achieved by the manipulation of one's environment by doing certain activities.

A complex interplay between both

Genetic and environmental factors combined often account for a lot of variation. Twin studies are a popular method of isolating genetic factors from environmental factors and vice versa. Monozygotic twins share the same genes, while dizygotic twins do not.

When an incidence of a certain condition, e.g. schizophrenia is higher between monozygotic twins compared to the general population, it can be deduced that a genetic component is accountable for the condition.

Genes may be responsible for one's weight, yet environmental factors like lifestyle, diet, exercise or surgery can change someone's weight and either bring it closer to the mean, or further away towards the extremes.

Structure of DNA

DNA (deoxyribonucleic acid) is a large molecule which carries the genetic information, or blueprint, of all life on Earth. Mutations arising in the DNA code account for the diversity upon which evolution by natural selection can work. Therefore, it is not far-fetched to say that DNA is one of the central, most important molecules in living organisms.

For such an important molecule, it sure looks beautiful:

False colour simulated DNA model

...actually, in reality it looks more like this:

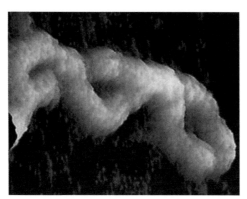

False colour DNA molecule

Pink candy floss anyone? The above image is a scanning electron micrograph, as you can see the 3D shape of DNA. The pink colour is likely due to a stain used.

DNA is a double helix i.e. two individual strands running along each other in an anti-parallel way, connected to one another by relatively weak hydrogen (H) bonds. DNA's structure can be learned easily by thinking about the strands and the "stuff in-between" separately.

What are the strands made of?

The strands are made of repeating units consisting of a deoxyribose (sugar) molecule with a phosphate molecule attached to it; hence, it is called a sugar-phosphate backbone.

What is the centre made of?

Attached to the sugar molecules in the backbone are a different type of molecule called nitrogenous base. There are 4 bases in DNA: adenine, thymine, cytosine and guanine. These are abbreviated by their initials: A, T, C and G.

The hydrogen bonds are formed between these bases. Due to their complementary shapes, A always pairs with T, and C always pairs with G. A-T is linked by 2 H bonds, while C-G is linked by 3. Here is a diagram of this arrangement:

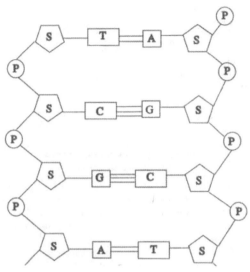

DNA backbone and bases

And another:

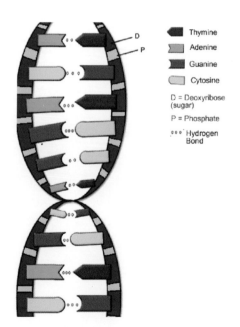

Structure of DNA (biologycorner.com)

DNA is a very stable molecule, as its purpose of carrying genetic information is very important. Features of this are:

1. DNA is very temperature-resistant, and the H bonds only break at temperatures of about 92 degrees Celsius

2. The sugar-phosphate backbone acts as a shield to the bases, preventing interference from outside chemical reactions

3. The double helix gives stability

4. Many H bonds contribute to the stability

5. The structure of the sugar-phosphate backbone itself confers strength

Genes and Polypeptides

It's important to distinguish between abstract concepts in biology, and actual physical things. DNA is deoxyribonucleic acid, a real molecule which can be viewed using an electron microscope, and which (were you very, very, very small) you could poke.

A gene, on the other hand, is just a location, called a locus (locus means location, all hail Latin!) on a specific strand of DNA, which contains the encoded information used to make a certain polypeptide which has a specific role in the development and function of an organism. This code is determined by the sequence of bases (A, T, C and G) at that location.

Think of a DNA strand like a bus garage. All buses look the same, they work the same (just like every adenine base is identical to the next adenine, and every thymine is just like the other thymine), yet every bus has a different number on it. This number is the "gene" - it is just a marker which determines where the bus will end up going once it's left the bus garage.

What a terrible example.

OK, try this:

ATCGTAGCAATATAGCGGATAGCGATGCTAGCGGCGTATAGGCTAGCTTAGGCATTG
CTCGATTAGCGGCCCATAGCT

AGGACATCGATCACACAGCTGGACTAGCTAGCTAGCTACACAGCTGAGACACACAGC
TATGCTAGAGCTAGGATCTG

AGATCTCACATTGCTATACAAGGCTAGGACTATAGCTTACAGACAGCAGACGACTGTC
TATATATATCGACATGCTAGT

AGCTTAGGCTATTAGCTATACAGACAGAATCGATACGACATATATGCGGCTATTACAG
ACGACATGACAGACATGACA

GCATTCTCGCGCGTAT**AGCGGCTATAGGCGCGATACGACTACG**AGAGAGATCGGACT
AGCGGCTACAGTCGGACAC

The above is just a tiny, tiny fraction of the sequence of bases in a DNA strand. Every 10 bases, the strand makes another full coil. Imagine it.

As any code, it translates into something. Every 3 consecutive bases may code for an amino acid. So the highlighted section may code for 9 amino acids, because there are 27 bases (27/3=9). These nine amino acids are the building blocks of a certain protein. The precise shape and 3D structure of this protein determines its function, and its function is what eventually makes us living things.

If as little as one error is made in a gene, for example a thymine replaces an adenine, the whole process may be disturbed to the point where debilitating diseases may result. Any change to the genetic code is a mutation. That sounds negative because, well, it is most of the time. Yet the odd mutations which result in positive effects that enhance survival and reproduction are precisely what evolution works on.

AGCGGCTATAGGCGCGATACG - let's assume this is a base sequence part of a gene responsible for haemoglobin.

AGCGGCTATAGGCGCTATACG - what's this?! Well, the same gene, but mutated. This is called an allele. It is a variant of a gene, the same gene which is responsible for haemoglobin.

Because the second allele has a T replacing the G, this may cause abnormal haemoglobin to be produced, which may result in Sickle cell disease. The name comes from the shape of red blood cells in affected people.

In eukaryotic organisms such as ourselves, most of the DNA doesn't code for polypeptides (proteins including enzymes). This is due to:

1. Repeats of the same sequences or genes, like AATTACAATTACAATTACAATTACAATTACAATTACAATTAC, and

2. Non-coding base sequences called introns.

Non-coding DNA is a bit like dark matter in physics. There's tons of it, it doesn't seem to do anything, yet it probably does a lot. Studies have suggested that non-coding DNA may contribute to the structural stability of DNA, provide plenty of error space (perhaps like experimenting ground?), act as a switch for certain genes, or promote the expression of some genes.

DNA and Chromosomes

DNA and chromosomes may seem like completely separate things. Well, they're not. In fact, all chromosomes are individual DNA molecules coiled and twisted around, because DNA is huge. At least in eukaryotes it is. That's one of the first differences between eukaryotes and prokaryotes in their DNA - prokaryotes have less DNA.

Eukaryotic DNA is stored within the nucleus of each cell (apart from cells without one, e.g. red blood cells). Because of its sheer size, it must be organised well. Proteins called histones help do just that:

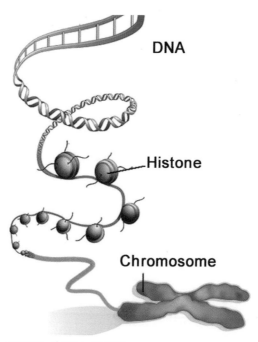

Wrapping of eukaryotic DNA

This is the second difference: eukaryotes have histones around which the DNA coils, while prokaryotes don't. So what does prokaryotic DNA look like?

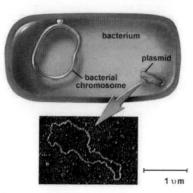

Bacterial plasmid

The DNA is stored as a small loop (the bacterial chromosome), and as a plasmid. A plasmid is even smaller, and may be copied and transferred to another bacterium of the same or different species by a process called conjugation (or, more colloquially, bacteria sex).

Eukaryotic DNA is linear, rather than circular. That means the DNA, despite being coiled numerous times, has a distinguishable start point and end point, while prokaryotic DNA is a continuous circle (see previous picture).

The Differences between Eukaryotic and Prokaryotic DNA

Size	large	small
Shape	linear	circular
Histones	present	absent

Meiosis

Meiosis is a type of cell division which results in four cells that are genetically non-identical from one parent cell. In order for one cell to divide to result in four cells, how many divisions must take place?

Two. One cell becomes two, then two become four:

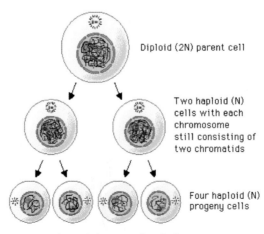

Overview of meiosis (Pearson Education)

The first division is called meiosis I, and the second is called meiosis II.

...so far so easy? (It should be!)

Cells resulting from meiosis are gametes such as egg cells and sperm cells, hence meiosis only occurs in sexually reproducing organisms. There are two key points about this:

1. Gametes are genetically unlike one another - while cells in other tissues such as muscle or blood must be genetically identical to one another (clones), the very basis of sexual reproduction is genetic diversity. So somewhere in the process of division, something takes place which creates genetic diversity (we'll come to that shortly).

2. If gametes are to fuse and result in a new organism, it is essential that the number of chromosomes should stay constant. Humans have 46 chromosomes in each cell (of course, apart from cells without DNA in them, and "spoiler alert!", gametes) - if each gamete had 46 chromosomes, then fusing two together would result in a zygote with 92 chromosomes, whose offspring would have 184 chromosomes, and before you know it something terrible would have happened.

The previous picture illustrates how the number of chromosomes is halved in the final four cells. The terms diploid and haploid refer to the number of sets of chromosomes. In humans, somatic cells (i.e. cells other than gametes) are diploid because there are two sets of chromosomes. Gametes are haploid because they have only one set of chromosomes.

A "set" is made up of all chromosomes which are unique, i.e. are not paired with any homologous chromosomes.

X x X X x X x x   <----------   haploid = 1 set

XX xx XX XX xx XX xx xx   <----------   diploid = 2 sets

In the first XX, X and X are homologous chromosomes because they occupy the same space and contain DNA with similar purpose/function. Essentially, they are more or less copies of each other. So when two gametes fuse, they form a diploid cell with the complete number of chromosomes.

Wikipedia does us the honour with this epic picture:

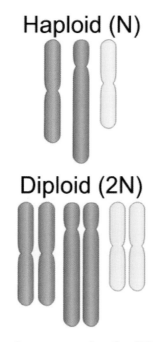

Chromosome configurations (Wikimedia Commons)

On to the very important bit now...

How does meiosis achieve genetic diversity without which you would actually look *just* like your siblings?

10 words: Independent Assortment of Homologous Chromosomes, & Genetic Recombination by Crossing Over

What an unnecessary mouthful. You still have to learn it though.

Independent assortment of homologous chromosomes means that in meiosis I, when the original diploid line-up a.k.a. XX xx XX XX xx XX xx xx becomes X x X X x X x x in 2 resulting cells, which big X's and which small x's end up with each other in each cell is random. Pretty simple concept.

XX xx

If you split the homologous chromosomes, you get Xx in two cells. The idea is that there is no rule saying that black must go with black, and red must go with red. You can end up with Xx and Xx, or Xx and Xx with an equal probability. What can I say, genetics likes being a bit random.

Genetic recombination by crossing over is a lot more interesting. It's like a bowl of spaghetti. Homologous chromosomes snuggle each other and exchange parts in the process:

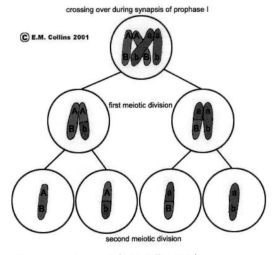

Crossing over in meiosis (E. M. Collins 2001)

Did I mention how important it is to use accurate scientific terminology in the exams? The process is called synapsis, during which mutual exchange of genetic information occurs.

Fascinating stuff.

As a finishing touch, I read of this mnemonic to remember the purpose of meiosis.

Makes

Eggs

In

Ovaries,

Sperm

In

Scrotum

It is so cringe-worthy, I would rather memorise meiosis off by heart.

Genetic Diversity

The genetic diversity between organisms is accounted for by variation in DNA. Even a tiny difference in DNA can result in a lot of variation. What's more, even identical DNA can still result in variation due to certain genes being active and others not. Is it visible that these two have largely identical DNA?

Chimp and human (James Balog)

Nope. Yet when compared to bacteria or an imaginary alien, those two above definitely look more closely related. So the similarities between human DNA and chimp DNA cause the visible and functional (phenotypical) similarities such as limbs, eyes, mouth, etc. while the differences in DNA result in the phenotypical differences such as hair thickness, facial features and so forth.

This knowledge has been used for a very long time by humans to manipulate wild plants and animals in order to make them somehow useful. People selectively breed plants and animals to change their genetic profile, so that certain traits are preferred over others.

Selective Breeding

Plants are selectively bred for higher yields, while animals are bred for many different purposes, such as food production, competitive events, aesthetic features, etc.

Selective breeding always leads to a decrease in variation. Overall, variation may increase as many different breeds are created - for example with dogs. Yet within one breed, variation is very low. There are ethical issues to be considered when selectively breeding animals. Dogs bred purely for cosmetic reasons, like Chihuahuas, can suffer from illnesses associated with their size, bone structure or facial features.

The Founder Effect

Suppose a boat travelled from one island to another. In the process, several lizards were transferred from the first island to the other. The lizards breed and settle down to form a new lizard population on their new island. This is called the founder effect. The small number of founding lizards formed the genetic base on which the whole population was built. This genetic base is significantly smaller than that of the original lizard population on the first island.

Therefore, the genetic diversity of the new population is lower than that of the original population.

Genetic Bottlenecks

The only difference between the founder effect and genetic bottlenecks is the way in which the new genetic pool is formed. In the founder effect the new pool is formed when a few individuals from a population become geographically isolated, while in genetic bottlenecks the new gene pool is formed when only a few individuals from a population survive a mass disaster, or are the only ones to breed.

The effect is the same: the genetic variation of the new population is decreased compared to the original population.

Haemoglobin

Haemoglobin is a type of protein. It is present in many varied organisms on our planet, and has a similar chemical structure in all of these organisms. In humans, haemoglobin is found in red blood cells. Haemoglobin's function is the transport of oxygen around the body. Oxygen must reach all parts of our bodies because it is required in the process of cellular respiration (to produce ATP - the main molecule involved in releasing energy for all uses).

Haemoglobin is a big deal, so naturally, it has a quaternary structure (multiple protein chains linked together to form a greater functional unit which also includes inorganic molecules). Just stare in awe at this beauty:

Structure of haemoglobin

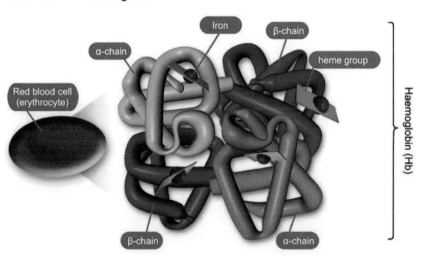

Each erythrocyte (RBC) contains ~270 million haemoglobin molecules

Components of haemoglobin

Erythrocyte is a very easy to remember name for a red blood cell. As you can see, there are four protein chains: two alpha chains and two beta chains. At the centre of each chain there is a haem (or heme) group which is an inorganic group containing one iron ion. The million pound question, of course, is how many iron ions are there in one haemoglobin molecule? (No, you will not be lucky enough to get that question for 10 marks in any exam.)

If you think this is all nice and easy, read on to be utterly disappointed.

Despite the fact that haemoglobins are similar in structure and function across a variety of organisms, they are adapted to different needs, as organisms span the large breadth of the biosphere. Some organisms need to be able to make use of very little oxygen available in their environment.

Since there are four iron ions in each haemoglobin molecule, and iron ions are directly responsible for binding the oxygen molecules (hence a lack of iron may cause anaemia), a haemoglobin molecule which has four oxygens bound to its haem groups is called saturated. The % saturation of haemoglobin overall in an organism is used to determine haemoglobin's ability to bind oxygen. This ability is affected by the partial pressure of oxygen (partial because it is only 21% of air).

This is a graph showing the oxygen dissociation curve:

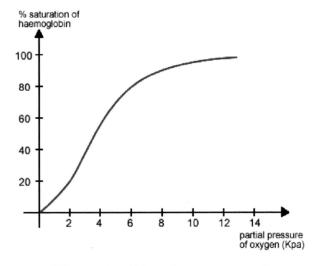

Haemoglobin saturation with increasing oxygen concentration

As you can see, the higher the partial pressure of oxygen (which reflects the amount of oxygen), the higher the % saturation of haemoglobin. Haemoglobin binds oxygen in the lungs where the partial pressure of oxygen is high. Of course, more oxygen than could be taken up by haemoglobin is irrelevant because the limiting factor becomes the number of haemoglobin molecules (hence the curve plateaus at about 8 KPa).

A very important point to take from the graph is that at a low partial pressure of oxygen (for example in respiring tissues), the % saturation of haemoglobin is decreasing. What this means is that haemoglobin has the unique ability to release oxygen where it is needed most. Abundance of oxygen in the lungs? Haemoglobin FETCHES! Tissues depleted of oxygen? Haemoglobin SPITS! Of course you will use terms such as oxygen binding and releasing, and percentage saturation of haemoglobin in your exams, won't you.

Let's go back to one of the first points on this topic. I said that haemoglobin action varies slightly between different organisms, depending on their individual needs and environment. This is a crucial point because those evil examiners will put a scary looking double, or even triple curve graph in front of you and ask you to explain what is going on. Looking at the previous graph, you can see that at 6 KPa the % saturation is 80. This may suit an organism fine, but others may well have shifted curves, where the points at which haemoglobin binds and releases oxygen are different. These curves may well be shifted to either the left or the right. This is what the graph might look like:

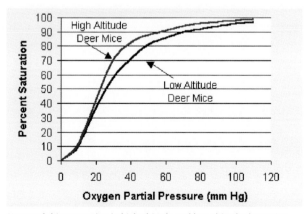

Haemoglobin saturation in high altitude and low altitude deer mice

If we take, say, 80% saturation, the corresponding partial pressure of oxygen is about 35 mm Hg for high altitude deer mice, and about 50 mm Hg for low altitude deer mice. What does this mean? It means that high altitude deer mice's haemoglobin binds oxygen at a lower partial pressure than that of low altitude deer mice. Essentially, their haemoglobin is able to make better use of less oxygen. Why?

Well, let's think, what do we know of these mice? Some live at high altitudes, and others live at low altitudes. What do we know about altitudes that is relevant? We know that there is less oxygen at higher altitudes in the atmosphere. Hence the haemoglobin of high altitude deer mice has evolved to bind oxygen at lower partial pressures - where there is less of it available. This confers a clear advantage in terms of survival.

Right, onto the last bit now (phew). You will be expected to know the effect of carbon dioxide (CO_2) on the oxygen dissociation curve. CO_2 being acidic decreases blood pH if in increasing quantity, and it results in carbamino compounds being produced. These compounds bind to haemoglobin and shift the curve to the right. Bicarbonate ions also contribute to a shift to the right, as they release protons into the blood plasma.

Carbohydrates

Starch

Basic unit: α glucose

Function: the main storage molecule in plants

Structure: starch is made of two compounds - amylose and amylopectin. Both are, of course, made of α glucose, but their overall shapes differ. Amylose is a spiral, while amylopectin has branches. Combined, they give starch the appearance of a tightly wound molecule like a brush.

Crucially, starch is an excellent storage compound, so must satisfy certain requirements. Its size must be relatively big so that it is not soluble. This prevents it from causing an osmotic effect in cells whereby water floods in. The molecule must be compact in order to take up little space rather than a lot. This is achieved by the branches and spirals within starch. Finally, the branches also contribute to the readiness of the glucose molecules to be "nipped off" and quickly usable. This is because only glucose molecules at the ends of starch can be used in that way.

Glycogen

Basic unit: α glucose

Function: the main storage carbohydrate in mammals

Structure: the structure of glycogen is essentially the same as that of amylopectin i.e. branched structure. The difference is that glycogen is even further branched compared to amylopectin. This enables a quicker build-up and breakdown of glycogen, hence meeting the superior energy demand of animals as compared with plants.

Cellulose

Basic unit: β glucose

Function: confers structural strength to plant cell walls

Structure: cellulose is the only molecule in this list which is solely made of β glucose. Despite beta glucose only having one chemical group different from alpha glucose, the result is a significant overall structural difference in cellulose. Unlike amylopectin and glycogen, cellulose has a structure based upon straight chains of beta glucose units, rather than spiralling chains of alpha glucose molecules.

These straight chains laid next to one another form hydrogen bonds which strengthen them into larger sub-units called microfibrils. Microfibrils are what cellulose is made of, and what gives plant cell walls their great strength.

Cells

The example for this topic will be (as per the specification) a palisade cell from a leaf. This is where palisade cells are located within a leaf:

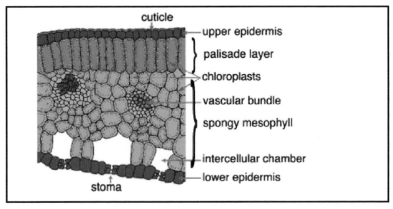

Components in leaf cross-section (Oregon State University)

They are just beneath the cuticle - very close to the leaf surface. You need to be familiar with the appearance of a palisade cell under an optical microscope. Without further ado, I present to you the stunning palisade cell:

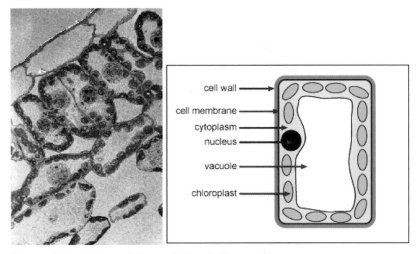

Micrograph of cells. Plant cell diagram (Wikimedia Commons)

Look at the black and white image. That is a micrograph of a leaf showing palisade cells along the surface. The blob in the centre that looks like a face is a palisade cell. The spheres lining its perimeter are chloroplasts. Can you spot the nucleus? Each palisade cell is surrounded by its cell wall which is made of cellulose.

The role of the cell wall is multi-fold:

1. Provides the plant with strength

2. Prevents the cell from bursting due to water flooding in by exerting pressure against the water flow

3. Gives tissues mechanical strength e.g. plants that rise high above the ground

4. Maintains the cell's specific shape

Just a quick break here. Why are we looking at palisade cells? Well, palisade cells are the ones containing copious amounts of chloroplasts. And chloroplasts contain all the substances and machinery necessary for photosynthesis. Without photosynthesis, you and I would not be here right now. Impressive. Take a closer look at this intricate organelle, the chloroplast, to whom we owe our lives:

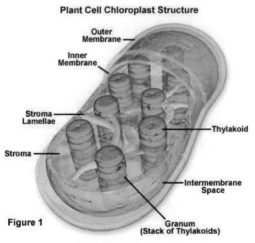

Chloroplast components (Michael W. Davidson)

www.thealevelbiologist.co.uk

This gooey mess whose constituent components have slightly uncommon and incredibly hard to memorise names is a chloroplast. Let's crunch them one by one.

Thylakoid, a disc-shaped organelle which contains chlorophyll (the lovely green pigment) rhymes with Kayla+Droid. Trust me, once you get the hang of this little word you will love it. Chlorophyll is involved in capturing sunlight (and the light dependent reaction). Multiple thylakoids stack together like towers within the chloroplast. A tower is called a granum, pl. grana. This arrangement enhances the surface area available.

The stroma is the fluid-filled space which is the site of the light-independent reaction.

The outer membrane and inner membrane are selectively permeable to allow O_2, CO_2, glucose and certain ions through.

Features which make chloroplasts well adapted to serve their function:

1. Chloroplasts are relatively flat and so ease the diffusion of molecules coming in and going out. This is achieved by a shorter diffusion pathway.

2. Plenty of available surface area for the reaction between chlorophyll and light to take place.

Now that wasn't so bad!

Replication of DNA

DNA, of course, replicates. Why? It's a pretty crucial element in the reproduction of living things. For example, a bacterium replicates by splitting itself into two (binary fission).

The DNA must stay intact and be copied with a high degree of accuracy in order for the two newly formed bacteria to develop and function as their parent - adequately. In multi-cellular organisms such as ourselves, DNA replication occurs as a prelude to cell division. You should already have read about meiosis.

For such a complex molecule, past scientists have had a challenging time working out the precise mechanism by which DNA replicates. Three hypotheses were made: (for this purpose imagine one DNA molecule)

1. The DNA molecule replicates by providing itself as a template for a brand new shiny DNA molecule, and then remaining its own intact DNA molecule. This is called the conservative replication model.

2. The DNA molecule replicates by providing itself as a template and being modified itself throughout, resulting in two new DNA molecules with patches of the old parent DNA molecule combined with patches of brand new material. This is called the dispersive replication model.

3. The DNA molecule replicates by providing each of its strands as a template for 2 new DNA molecules, each having one entire new strand, and one entire old strand from the parent DNA molecule. This is called the semi-conservative replication model.

Here's a visual aid for those who found the above descriptions gibberish:

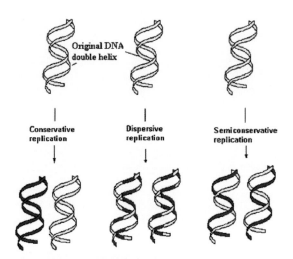

Past DNA replication hypotheses

How does one go about working out which one of these models is the correct one? Well, in the '50s these two chaps by the names of Meselson and Stahl cracked the riddle by carrying out a classic experiment which the examiners are in love with (so learn it well).

Now that we're all clear on the replication model of DNA, let's delve deeper into the details of the process. These are the key steps involved in the semi-conservative replication of DNA:

1. The enzyme DNA helicase unwinds the double helix, causing the hydrogen bonds between the two polynucleotide strands to break.

2. DNA-binding proteins maintain the two strands separate during replication.

3. Enzymes called primases attach primers to the exposed strand. Primers are a few nucleotides long and constitute the site where DNA polymerase starts its action.

4. DNA polymerase binds to the aforementioned primer and begins catalysing the reaction between free nucleotides (new) and DNA-bound nucleotides (old). Of course this complies with the principle of complementarity i.e. A-T, C-G.

Mitosis

Multi-cellular organisms such as ourselves are... multi-cellular. This point must be emphasised in learning about mitosis because mitosis is the process by which this is possible. A bacterium is a cell which divides to produce two bacteria, yet that cell is the organism itself. Multi-cellular organisms require a process by which one cell divides into two, those two into four, and so forth, until a gargantuan number of cells come alive. Cells are organised in tissues (such as skeletal muscle), tissues are organised in organs (such as the skin), and organs are organised into systems (such as the nervous system). The various systems make up the live organism.

Overview of Mitosis

Mitosis is the process by which cells divide to achieve growth and repair by simply increasing cell number. The dividing cell is called the parent cell, and the resulting two cells are called progeny cells. The progeny cells are genetically identical i.e. clones, as they contain copies of the parent cell's DNA.

Stages of Mitosis

Prophase, metaphase, anaphase, telophase and cytokinesis.

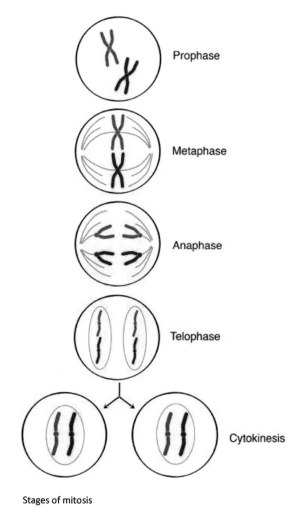

Stages of mitosis

Prophase

1. Chromosomes begin to appear visible under a microscope due to chromatin (the coiled and yet-again coiled DNA fibre) condensing. Before this the DNA is not specifically distinguishable in the shape of chromosomes. This is a terrible word tangle so this is how it is. From a bowl of spaghetti (the nucleus) put the spaghetti in the shape of several chromosomes. Chromatin is the spaghetti initially, and chromosomes are the spaghetti still, just turned and twisted and distinguishable as individual stick-shaped objects. That is all, that's all it is. Before this happens though, the DNA must be replicated - that's the reason behind the X shape of chromosomes; they are two "lines" a.k.a. chromatids joined together at their centres called centromeres.

2. The nuclear envelope breaks down.

3. Organelles known as centrioles migrate towards the poles of the cell. These organelles are involved in the act of pulling the chromosomes apart into the soon-to-be progeny cells. They achieve this by the microtubules that extend out of them and connect to the centromeres. Microtubules are like lassos. Sort of.

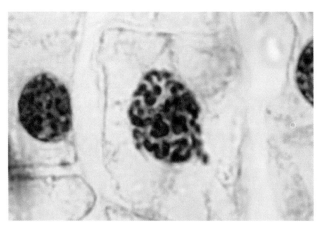

Prophase

Metaphase

Chromosomes are aligned at the cell equator by spindle fibres (made of the aforementioned microtubules) which lengthen and shorten themselves on opposing sides (tug of war) until all chromosomes are lined up about halfway across the cell. This area is called the metaphase plate. It looks like a plate. Who said biology can't be straightforward?

Metaphase

Anaphase

The chromatids split at their centromeres and are pulled towards opposite poles of the cell by the shortening spindle fibres.

Anaphase (Michael W. Davidson)

Telophase

1. Nuclear envelopes reform around the two new nuclei.

2. The chromosomes decondense and become indistinguishable under a microscope yet again, and the spindle fibres spread out.

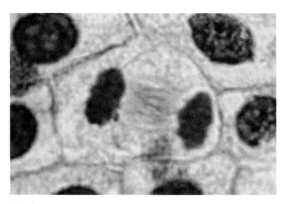

Telophase

Cytokinesis

This is the final step of mitosis when the cytoplasm of the parent cell divides to complete the cell division, resulting in two brand new and individual progeny cells.

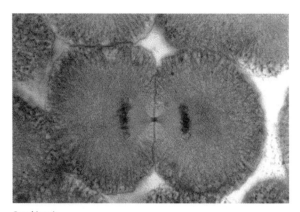

Cytokinesis

Cell Cycle

The cell cycle refers to the distinct stages through which a cell goes, from the moment it becomes a cell to the moment it divides to result in two separate cells.

It starts with gap 1, G1, continues into the S phase (S is for synthesis) where DNA replicates, followed by gap 2, G2, and ends with mitosis.

G1 and G2 may sound like codes for some complex enzymes, but they are mere notations for gaps 1 and 2, which are just that: gaps between mitosis and DNA replication (in the S phase) respectively. G1 through to G2 - that's G1, S phase and G2 - are all stages which collectively are known as interphase. Inter = between; phase = ...phase, so interphase is just the stage between a cell's creation and that cell's division by mitosis.

Interphase is by far the stage in which most cells are in most of the time. The other stage, the small one, is called the mitotic phase and it encompasses mitosis (prophase, metaphase, anaphase and telophase) plus cytokinesis.

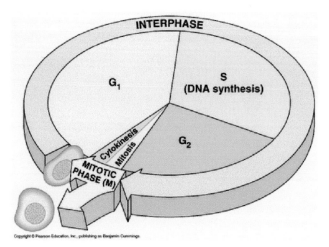

Overview of the cell cycle (Pearson Education)

Knowledge of the cell cycle comes in very useful in the treatment of cancer. Cancerous cells divide out of control, often due to mutations in DNA which result in improper regulation of cell division. These mutations have been isolated in certain genes known as oncogenes. The best drugs to treat cancer must be efficient at targeting and killing the cancerous cells, without damaging any nearby healthy cells. When cells divide too quickly, tumour suppressor genes regulate them and give DNA an opportunity to be repaired, or for the immune response to kill the cancerous cells. If the tumour suppressor genes mutate themselves, then the probability of cancer developing increases significantly.

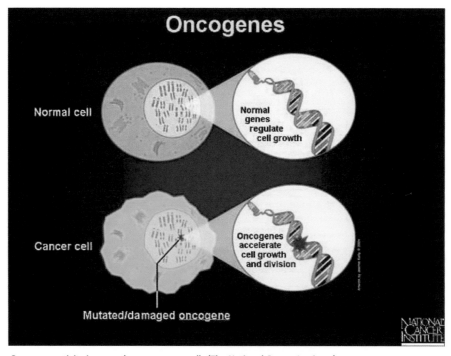

Oncogene activity in normal versus cancer cells (The National Cancer Institute)

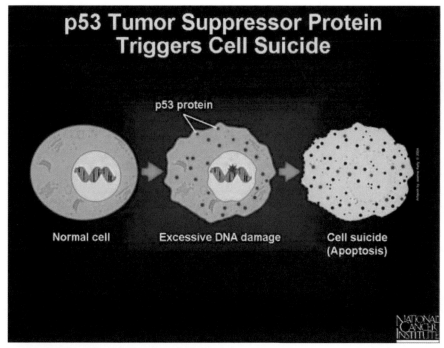

Cell suicide pathway (The National Cancer Institute)

Lovely little topic. Remember the stage of the cell cycle where DNA replicates (interphase → S phase). Also, some cells never undergo mitosis, and so remain in G1 indefinitely. In this particular scenario the cells are said to be in the G0 phase.

Cell Differentiation

All of the cells in your body, every single last cell, can be traced back to just a single cell (the fertilised egg a.k.a. zygote), and a single DNA code. How is it possible for hundreds of different cell types to arise from that? The zygote undergoes mitosis, and according to that, all progeny cells resulting are genetically identical. Therefore, all cells in our body must be genetically identical. Well, they are*. So how do all these supposed "clone cells" end up being so different from one another, and hence achieve such different purposes within the larger organism?

They differentiate due to selected genes becoming active in certain cells but not others. The initial cells from which others can differentiate are called stem cells. These can be totipotent, pluripotent or unipotent. Totipotent stem cells have the ability to differentiate into any type of cell. Pluripotent stem cells are descendants of totipotent stem cells, and can differentiate into many different kinds of cell, but not all. Unipotent stem cells can only replicate themselves, and so produce just one type of cell.

The genes active in cells determine whether they are skin cells, heart muscle cells, neurons, lung cells, etc.

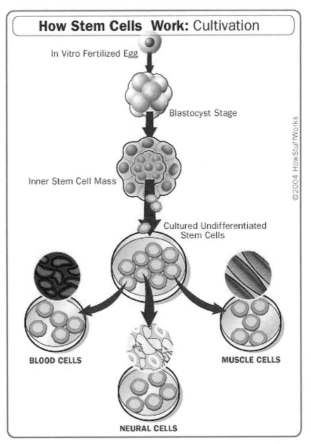

Stem cell applications from embryonic stem cells (HowStuffWorks)

A tissue is formed of structurally and functionally similar cells. For example, nerve tissue or connective tissue.

An organ is formed of multiple tissues working to achieve a physiological function. For example, the pancreas is involved in blood glucose regulation.

A system is formed of multiple organs which achieve an overarching function in an organism. For example, the circulatory system ensures a constant blood supply around the body.

*Of course you must have worked out so far that biology is never that simple. Somatic cells (i.e. most cells in our body, with gametes - eggs and sperm - excluded) are theoretically clones. Gametes arise from meiosis rather than mitosis, hence they are all very diverse genetically. Spontaneous mutations can arise in some somatic cells, say, in one cell in your knee. That mutation has just made that cell cease to be a clone, or genetically identical, to the other cells. By and large, though, the majority of cells in the body are clones.

Size and Surface Area

Organisms exchange substances and heat with their environment all the time, and this possibility is crucial to survival. The specific way in which this is achieved is very tightly related to the shape and structure of the specific organism, as well as its environment. For example, unicellular organisms are so small that molecules such as oxygen and water can readily diffuse in and out via the membrane, due to the short diffusion pathway. Could this be achieved by a human, or even a bee? No - they are simply too big.

Two properties are important to consider here: the volume of an organism, and the surface area of an organism. The volume is what determines the amount of substances which need exchanging, while the surface area determines the amount which can be exchanged. Key principle: as the size of an organism increases, the surface area to volume ratio decreases.

That might seem hard to really understand. Why use a ratio in the first place? Well, the ratio shows the relationship between surface area and volume, i.e. how similar or dissimilar are they?

Cube volume changes greatly with surface area

Maths Time

Small cube
Surface area = 1^2 x 6 = 6
Volume = 1^3 = 1
Surface area: volume = 6:1 = **6.00**

Big cube
Surface area = 2^2 x 6 = 24
Volume = 2^3 = 8
Surface area: volume = 24:8 = 3:1 = **3.00**

3 is smaller than 6, so as the cube/organism gets larger, the surface area to volume ratio decreases.

What this basically means is that the larger an organism gets, the less surface area is available to serve its increasing needs due to its increasing volume. So what adaptations do larger organisms have to cope with the large demand for substance and heat exchange?

For one, mere diffusion directly into and out of the organism is not possible. Insects, for example, have a system of tubules which distribute air within the body so that it reaches all the different parts. Mammals have lungs and blood vessels. Fish have gills. All these systems are specifically aimed at making it possible to exchange substances such as oxygen, carbon dioxide and nutrients as well as heat, between an organism and its environment.

In fact, the reason behind insects' limited size is that their tubule system can only work for those sizes. Otherwise, we might just have gigantic wasps flying around. Be thankful for surface area to volume ratio!

Gas Exchange

Single-celled Organisms

Since gas exchange occurs by diffusion alone, single-celled organisms such as bacteria do not need any specialised structures to achieve it for them. This is because, being so small, diffusion occurs readily as their surface area to volume ratio is high.

The distance between an oxygen molecule which must be taken in, and the place it must get to within a bacterium is short enough for diffusion to be a viable way of exchanging substances with the environment, without the need for additional structures. In mammals, for example, oxygen cannot simply diffuse into our bodies. We are too large, have a low surface area to volume ratio, hence the diffusion pathway is too long. The only way we can achieve gas exchange is through our lungs which provide a large surface area and alveoli with short diffusion pathways.

In fact, the difficulty of gas exchange as single-celled organisms get larger is a factor which leads to larger organisms being multicellular.

Insects

Before this goes any further, a few clarifications:

1. Gas exchange is central to life. Oxygen is needed in respiration* which generates usable energy without which life wouldn't exist. Removing the resulting carbon dioxide is crucial too.

2. Water can be a gas too, in the form of water vapour. This may in certain organisms escape with the air, so water preservation versus gas exchange is always an important thing to bear in mind. This is especially important when talking about insects and plants.

Insects have a tracheal system made up of many tracheae which branch into smaller tracheoles. All tracheae connect to the exoskeleton of the insect, so that air diffuses in and out through the spiracles.

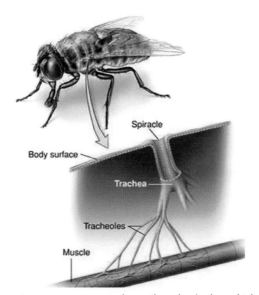

Insects carry out gas exchange through spiracles and tubules (McGraw-Hill)

These technical terms are important in describing what really is just a bunch of holes and tubes.

In order to balance the opposing needs for conserving water and obtaining oxygen, insects are able to close their spiracles, as well as contract their abdomens. The former prevents water loss, while the latter enhances ventilation so that more oxygen gets inside their body.

Fish

Fish extract dissolved oxygen molecules from the surrounding water. The oxygen content of water is much lower compared to air, so fish have special adaptations which enable them to make the most of the available oxygen. These adaptations are gills.

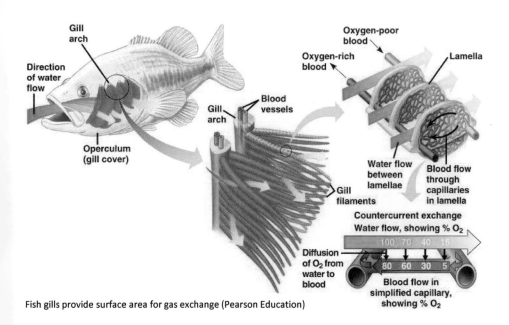

Fish gills provide surface area for gas exchange (Pearson Education)

Key points:

1. Gill filaments have lamellae which increase the surface area available for diffusion, while keeping the diffusion pathway short.

2. The water flow through the fish's mouth as well as the blood in gill capillaries follow the countercurrent principle. As seen in the previous diagram, water and blood flow against each other, rather than along each other. This ensures that oxygen diffusion can take place along the whole length of the flow, not just for half of it - before the concentrations of oxygen in the blood and in the water become equal.

This is easily exemplified (and an acceptable form of explanation in an exam) by a number table. The upper row is the oxygen concentration in the blood, while the lower is the one in the water. Along the flow, oxygen enters the bloodstream from the water, so that the concentration in blood increases, while the concentration in water decreases.

```
-------------------------------->
0  1  2  3  4  5  6  7  8  9        - deoxygenated blood becomes oxygen-rich
^  ^  ^  ^  ^  ^  ^  ^  ^  ^        - oxygen from the water enters the bloodstream
1  2  3  4  5  6  7  8  9 10
<--------------------------------
```

If water flowed in the same direction as blood, this is what it would look like:

```
-------------------------------->
0  1  2  3  4  5  5  5  5  5        - deoxygenated blood slightly oxygenated, stalls
^  ^  ^  ^  ^                      -diffusion stops when concentrations are equal
10 9  8  7  6  5  5  5  5  5
-------------------------------->
```

Plants

Like insects, plants must meet the opposing demands of water retention and gas exchange. The site of photosynthesis in plants, as well as the gas exchange site, is the leaf. This is what a section through a leaf looks like (not really, this is just a diagram):

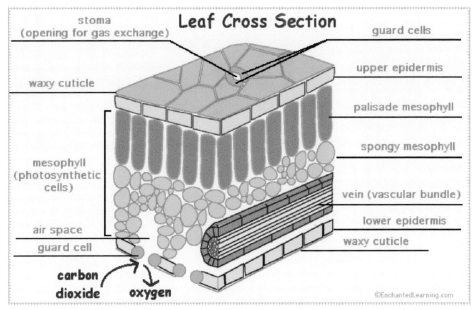

Components of leaves (EnchantedLearning.com)

If you wish to learn all the names, you are more than welcome, and crazy in a good way. These are the bits you must focus on:

1. The mesophyll cells are surrounded by quite a lot of empty space for air to mingle around, providing plenty of surface area for gas exchange by diffusion.

2. Air with its carbon dioxide (necessary for photosynthesis) enters the leaf through the stomata. Stomata are holes on the leaf surface, made by the guard cells. They can open and close depending on environmental factors such as humidity, temperature and wind. This controls the amount of water loss. Oxygen, the by-product of photosynthesis, also leaves the leaf through the stomata.

*Biology is basically an endless sequence of asterisks. Sigh. Oxygen is needed in aerobic respiration, as opposed to anaerobic respiration. Biology is a beautiful, flexible and volatile thing with endless possibilities. On Earth, by and large, respiration requires oxygen. But is it possible to have respiration without oxygen? Certainly. Now imagine what there is out there, in the universe...

Mass Transport

Gas exchange in large multicellular organisms is achieved by organs which have a large surface area and so are able to successfully provide the substances the organism needs in order to survive. In humans this is achieved by the lungs, but how does the oxygen acquired by the lungs actually reach every single cell of the body? A network of sorts is needed to do that. Many bigger and smaller tubes would come in handy. They would form like a... circulatory system. Oh wait, that's precisely what mammals have: a circulatory system made of arteries, veins, capillaries, etc.

Plants, too, have a vascular (tubular) system. It is made of xylems and phloems. Yes, complicated names which you will love to learn about in the following topic (The Passage of Water through a Plant).

The key thing is that this circulation of a large amount of substances via a system of transportation is called mass flow, hence mass transport. Just more technical terms for you to learn, which describe something that really couldn't get any simpler. Water and gases chillin' through tubes in an organism.

The Blood System

Cells in mammals require a constant supply of nutrients and oxygen, and a way to remove waste products. Blood is great, as it does all that. Blood needs a way of getting to all cells of the body, a way to... circulate. Without that, blood would just get pulled by gravity towards the centre of the earth. Not a pretty sight I'm afraid.

There are two circulations in the body:

1. The pulmonary circulation takes blood from the heart, pumping it to the lungs in order to oxygenate it.

2. The systemic circulation takes blood from the heart to everywhere else. Eyes, legs, hands, bum, you name it.

Key point: the oxygen-rich blood vessels entering an organ are called arteries, while the oxygen-depleted blood vessels leaving an organ are called veins.

So a blood vessel entering the liver or kidneys would be an artery. A blood vessel leaving the liver or kidneys would be a vein.

The liver attribute is hepatic (for example, the working cell unit in the liver is the hepatic cell), while the kidney attribute is renal (for example, renal failure). So what would the blood vessel entering the liver be called?

...pressing question.

...pressing on.

...

...the hepatic artery! Same principle applies to the rest: the hepatic vein, the renal artery and the renal vein.

There's a catch (welcome to biology). In the case of the blood vessels leaving or entering the lungs, the rules are reversed. The pulmonary vein carries oxygenated blood to the heart, while the pulmonary artery carries deoxygenated blood into the lungs.

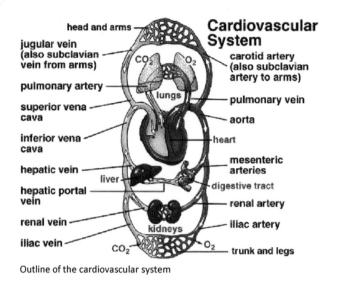

Outline of the cardiovascular system

You also need to learn the blood vessels entering and leaving the heart.

1. The aorta is the main artery which carries oxygen-rich blood to the rest of the body.

2. The coronary arteries supply blood to the heart itself (and they are the affected arteries in coronary heart disease).

3. The superior vena cava and the inferior vena cava bring deoxygenated blood from the upper half of the body, and the lower part of the body respectively.

It's all really logical... apart from the bit on the lungs.

There are four types of blood vessels: arteries, arterioles, capillaries and veins. Each type has a different function, and therefore a different structure. Here is a diagram of how arteries branch off into arterioles, then into capillaries, and eventually into veins as the blood becomes deoxygenated.

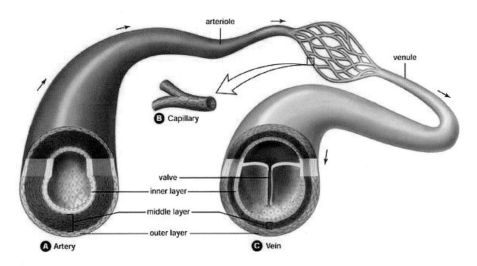

Figure 9.12. Sections through an artery, capillary, and vein. At any given moment, about 30% of the blood in your systemic circulation will be found in the arteries, 5% in the capillaries, and 65% in the veins.

Differences between arteries and veins

Function

So what do they do?

Arteries must be able to counteract the pressure created by every heart beat by recoiling, so that the stream of blood is smoothened.

Arterioles are able to direct blood supply to certain parts of the body, so must be able to constrict or dilate.

Capillaries are the site of substance exchange as well as diffusion, so their walls must be thin enough for this to happen quickly.

Veins are unique as they contain valves which prevent backflow of blood.

Structure

From the previous picture is it clear that there are important structural differences between arteries and veins, which reflect their different functions. Firstly, veins have valves while arteries do not. Secondly, arteries have a narrower lumen (hollow diameter) than veins. Thirdly, arteries have a thicker wall of muscle and elastic tissue.

Arteries and arterioles are similar. The key difference is that arteries have more elastic tissue than muscle, while arterioles have more muscle than elastic tissue.

Capillaries are 1-cell thick, making them very thin and permeable.

Tissue Fluid

Tissue fluid is what surrounds all respiring cells. This is where they draw their nutrients from, and where they eliminate waste products into. Tissue fluid movement back and forth between cells and blood is directed by one of two things: either the hydrostatic pressure exerted by the blood rushing through arteries; or by osmosis caused by the proteins within blood.

Therefore, as blood goes through the artery to respiring tissues, the tissue fluid is forced out of the blood, into the tissues. As blood passes through, it loses pressure so that the tissue fluid now enters the subsequent vein due to osmosis. This occurs because the water potential in the vein is lower than outside due to the proteins in the blood which reduce it. This sums up the circulation of tissue fluid.

The Passage of Water through a Plant

Water enters a plant through the roots. In order to understand how water gets in the root, you should definitely check out the root structure:

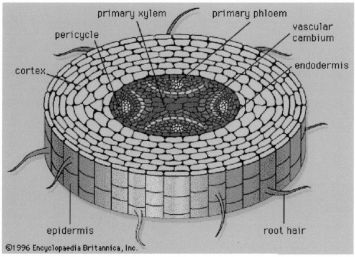

Components of root cross-section (Encyclopaedia Britannica)

What you can see above is a delicious slice of pineapple. OK, it's not. That is a slice of a root. Roots, as you may have seen in real life, are hairy. All those tiny and not so tiny root hairs buried into the soil greatly increase the surface area of the root. This exposes it to more water molecules which can be taken up. The hairs are nothing like human hairs; they are extensions of the outer layer of the root, made up of cells. This layer is called the epidermis.

Why does water move inside the root? Simple: osmosis. The cell sap (i.e. cell juice) has a lower water potential than the fluid found in the soil, so the water in the soil kindly makes its way into the thirsty awaiting root. Once the water reaches the first cell in its path, the water potential of that cell is increased compared to the cell next to it. Therefore, water moves into the next cell, leaving the current cell. This in turn results in the previous cell taking up water all over again, and so forth, until water makes its way across all cells of the cortex.

Reaching the endodermis, water then enters the xylem. The xylem is a tissue of dead cells which contributes to the vascular system of plants by being the transportation medium for water and dissolved mineral ions. The xylem brings them to the leaves and other organs.

There are two different pathways that water uses in order to reach the xylem:

1. The apoplast pathway whereby water slaloms between cell walls and the spaces in between, without passing directly through live tissue; this accounts for 90% of water uptake.

2. The symplast pathway whereby water goes straight through living tissue i.e. the cells in the cortex, and into the xylem; this accounts for only 10% of water uptake.

Basically, the symplast pathway is just way simpler.

Transpiration

Transpiration is water loss through the parts of a plant which are found above soil level i.e. not the roots. As water streams through a plant, transpiration affects the speed of the stream. Increased transpiration will lead to a quicker uptake of water through the roots to maintain the water flow throughout the plant. So what affects transpiration?

1. Light causes stomata to open, resulting in increased water loss (transpiration)

2. Temperature going up also raises the rate of transpiration, as more water molecules evaporate

3. Humidity. An increase in humidity around the leaves means that there is less space for water molecules from the plant to evaporate into, so transpiration is decreased

4. Air movement (wind) can displace water molecules from around the stomata, so that more space becomes available for additional water molecules to go into; transpiration increases

Root pressure. The cohesion-tension hypothesis

These are the two ways in which the stream of water through a plant can work. Root pressure is the water being pushed into the roots, while cohesion-tension is the water being pulled up.

When a plant doesn't transpire much, mineral ions can accumulate at the bottom in the roots. This decreases the water potential inside the roots, so that water moves in by osmosis from the soil into the roots.

A key property of water is cohesion. Cohesion refers to the way in which water molecules stick to one another. A good example of this is when water moves up a very narrow plastic tube, all by itself. This is due to water sticking to itself and hence pulling itself upwards. This happens in plants too.

Principles of Taxonomy

Taxonomy refers to the classification of living things by giving unique names to each species, and creating a hierarchy based on evolutionary descent. This is a challenging task, as most species that have ever lived on this planet are now extinct, and many more alive today have yet to be discovered and classified.

In order to achieve that, we need a definition for both species and hierarchy. In the old days, a species was known as a collection of individuals similar enough in resemblance to be put in the same box. This was purely based on physical features. Today we know that similar physical characteristics on their own aren't enough to define a species.

A species is defined in terms of observable physical features as well as the ability to produce fertile offspring.

Liger Hercules: the product of different species

This is Hercules, the liger. Hercules has a lion father and a tiger mother. Does that mean tigers and lions are really one species? This is one example of the issues surrounding both the definition of species, and taxonomy generally.

What is a hierarchy? A hierarchy, put simply, is a system of classification comprised of small groups contained within larger groups contained within larger groups, and so forth, where there is no overlap.

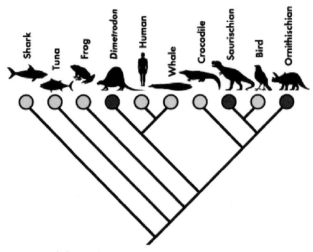

Summary phylogenetic tree

This diagram is a phylogenetic tree. It is a representation of various species in terms of their genetic relatedness. Each "crossroad" is a different ancestor. From this diagram it is easy to see that humans are more closely related to whales than to birds, or indeed any other species represented.

The species with a red circle beneath are extinct. If a phylogenetic tree were made with all species that have ever lived up to today, the vast majority would be extinct.

The names in the diagram are used for convenience, yet the scientifically correct way of classifying organisms is by giving them a two-word (binomial) name. These names are in Latin or Greek.

Let's take *Homo sapiens* for example (us!):

1. It's written in italics as all species names should be, by convention.

2. It's made up of two words: Homo and sapiens.

3. Homo denotes the genus to which the species belongs to. A genus is the group higher than species. For example, *Homo erectus* and *Homo neanderthalensis* are part of the same genus as *Homo sapiens*. That genus is called Homo... getting the hang of it?

4. Sapiens denotes the species itself, and is the smallest group in the hierarchy.

What does the rest of the hierarchy look like?

Kingdom, Phylum, Class, Order, Family, Genus, Species (fearing you can't possibly remember this sequence?)

Kinky, Policemen, Can, Often, Find, Gay, Sex. You're more than welcome.

Genetic Comparisons

More reliable and accurate than mere physical resemblance in determining the genetic relationship between individuals and species, is of course a genetic comparison. This can be achieved by directly analysing their DNA or the proteins encoded by it.

DNA Comparisons

There is a correlation between the degree of relatedness between individuals/species, and the degree of similarity between their base sequences in DNA. For example, ACTGGAC and ACTGGAT are more similar than ACTGGAC and GCTGGAA. Hence, it may be deduced that the organism possessing the first sequence is more closely related to the second organism, than to the last organism.

One technique which enables scientists to carry out a DNA comparison is called DNA hybridisation. This involves the joining together of DNA sections from two species to be compared. These are the steps involved:

1. DNA samples are collected, cut into smaller sections, and then heated to 90 degrees.

2. The heat denatures the DNA molecules by breaking the hydrogen bonds within; the strands of DNA separate.

3. The separated strands from the two species are now put together and allowed to cool.

4. Some strands will join back with their original pair; others will join with strands from the other organism to form hybrid DNA.

The temperature at which these strands re-anneal (bond together) is the clue to the genetic relationship between the two organisms. DNA strands which join back with their original counterpart from the same organism re-anneal at 87 degrees, as they share a lot of base sequences. The hybrid DNA, on the other hand, is formed at a lower temperature. This is because fewer sequences are shared, and so fewer hydrogen bonds are formed which hold the strands together.

The lower the temperature at which hybrid DNA forms between two organisms, the less genetically related they are. This technique has led to a new classification system being used for plants.

Protein (Amino Acid) Comparisons

Proteins are sequences of amino acids. The exact sequence of amino acids found in a protein in an organism may differ from one to another, usually between different species. Whether it differs, and the degree to which it does, suggests how closely related those organisms/species are.

The sequence may be identical, different by one amino acid, or different by 50 amino acids. This information is very helpful in building phylogenetic trees, especially as there are so many different proteins which can be analysed to build a complete picture.

Courtship Behaviour

What is courtship behaviour? The acts it encompasses are as varied as life itself; a sound, a gesture, an action, etc. The overarching and general attribute all these behaviours have (which makes them courtship) is whether they appear to be connected to successful mating.

The first feature of courtship behaviour is that it enables organisms to identify members of their own species. The central part of the definition of a species is the members' ability to produce viable offspring. Hence, attempting to mate with members of a different species is not an advantageous behavioural trait in the context of reproductive success.

Courtship behaviours also allow organisms to approach one another without aggression or invasion of their personal space.

Sometimes the outcome of courtship behaviour is the formation of a pair bond. This bond results in a better reproductive success, due to the increased survival probability of the offspring. In some species this is the case, while in others it isn't. This is tightly related to a specific organism's physiology. Fish are able to lay a huge number of eggs, while pigeons only lay one or two. Therefore, it is more likely that pigeons would from a pair bond, rather than fish.

Last, but by no means least, is the nature of courtship behaviour which makes it a tool for sexual selection. This is not a mere test of survival (natural selection takes care of that), but a test of relative superiority in a variety of attributes which vary between species, at different times, and even between individual organisms. These attributes can be anything, and in many cases they seem random or peculiar. In others, they seem very much expected.

Antibiotics

Antibiotics is one of those technical terms in biology which actually describes its object. ANTI = against, BIOTIC = life. So antibiotics are weapons of mass destruction... sort of.

They are substances which occur both naturally, as well as artificially as made by humans. The reason they are so widespread and important is because they solve a problem humanity has had for a very long time (i.e. forever). They are used to treat bacterial infections. Today that might seem like a small thing, yet around the globe millions of people still die all the time due to bacterial infections (e.g. pneumonia). It's not a small thing, it is one of the greatest medical discoveries.

A one-week course of antibiotics taken orally, for example, can easily treat bacterial infections and the associated disease. This is an amazing achievement. Antibiotics are substances which kill prokaryotic cells, such as bacteria, while leaving eukaryotic cells (in humans and others) untouched.

Each type of antibiotic targets different things in bacteria. One of the main differences between bacterial and human cells is that the former have a cell wall, while the latter don't. Some antibiotics prevent the formation of cell walls. This renders the bacteria vulnerable to water flooding inside and bursting them. Burst bacteria can't replicate (really?), and hence the infection ceases.

This is called osmotic lysis. Lysis means breaking or disintegration, while osmotic refers to the osmotic effect which results in water flooding into the bacteria, from higher water potential (outside the bacteria) to lower water potential (inside the bacteria).

Other ways in which antibiotics target and kill bacteria include interfering with their DNA replication, so they can't replicate further, and interfering with their protein synthesis. This essentially blocks the normal running of their metabolic functions, rendering them dead or unable to replicate.

Genetic Variation in Bacteria

(1) Genetic - why? All of the characteristics of bacterial organisms are a result of the blueprint for the various proteins coded in their DNA, the same DNA that all life has on Earth (except for the specific base sequence). Genetic simply means arising from DNA.

(2) Variation - bacteria have variation? Who would have thought? I mean, I always thought they were just a bunch of tiny hot dogs without the sausage in the middle, hanging around causing trouble. Well, I found out, no, they're not hot dogs. They're beautiful organisms in their own right, and if it weren't for our inherent bias of being on the receiving end of their infection, they wouldn't be baddies. They could be heroes. In fact, some of them are heroes! Some bacteria do contribute positively to our life. The undeniable evidence for that is pickles.

(1+2) So, the variation is genetic.

(3) Bacteria - why bacteria? Due to bacteria being a common cause of disease, as well as their fast life cycle, they are a good case study for explaining selection and resistance. This is done in the light of antibiotic resistance. Things are complicated on Earth; in the Antibiotics topic I point out that antibiotics literally murder bacteria in a very efficient way. What could go wrong?

As generations of bacteria come to life, their DNA doesn't stay completely identical. Random mutations sometimes arise. Mutations are changes in DNA which result in different characteristics. No, not bacteria with fangs, but subtle changes in, say, the shape of a certain protein which sits on the cell wall. These mutations and the bacteria don't "know" which, or if, these changes will turn out favourable or unfavourable. This depends on their environment. Some mutations may even be irrelevant or neutral.

The key point is that sometimes, some bacteria develop mutations which just so happen to give them resistance to an antibiotic.

This resistance, being genetic, is passed on to the offspring by vertical transmission (bacteria dividing; called binary fission - which literally means splitting in two). It's called vertical because it happens from top to bottom, as multiple generations arise.

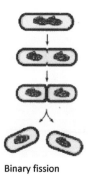

Binary fission

As you can see, this happens "vertically". In reality, there is no such thing as vertical. Bacteria divide any which way, clearly. But silly humans can't understand the concept of no direction... A way of looking at it is that the transmission only occurs if the given bacterium divides.

In horizontal transmission, the given bacterium doesn't divide. It exchanges genetic material from its plasmid (circular bit of DNA) by replicating the plasmid and passing it along via a tube to a different bacterium, even of another species.

This process is called conjugation, and many a cheeky teacher have compared it to sex.

F-factor Transfer

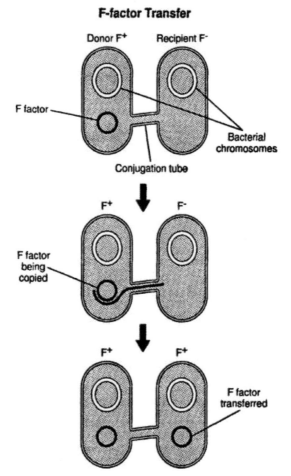

Horizontal DNA transfer between bacteria

No worries about the F factor (it's the factor which enables the receiving bacterium to initiate conjugation).

In the picture think of the plasmid - the black circle being copied and transferred - as a bit of DNA which contains the allele responsible for antibiotic resistance. Now the other fellow has it. Damn.

If out of a million bacteria, just one lone bacterium happens by chance to have an allele that confers it resistance to the antibiotic used, then that bacterium will survive. Replicate. To a million antibiotic-resistant bacteria. See the problem now?

It's not even started. Now all of the million bacteria are resistant, and can pass on the resistance to bacteria of other species by conjugation. Now... see the catastrophe? Sooner rather than later, that particular antibiotic will be rendered useless. This is a real world problem, resulting in many strains of bacteria being untreatable, for example in tuberculosis and MRSA. MRSA stands for Methicillin-Resistant *Staphylococcus Aureus*. Methicillin is a sort of antibiotic from the penicillin class. *Staphylococcus Aureus* is a species of bacteria. And they're resistant. MRSA is a big issue in hospitals.

This issue can be managed, yet irresponsible use of antibiotics makes it worse. This includes:

1. Doctors over-prescribe antibiotics, when they are not necessary, or in case of viral infections (viruses aren't killed by antibiotics).

2. Patients don't finish their full course of antibiotics. This leaves the strongest bacteria alive, and gives them a chance to breed, resulting in a population of bacteria which is more antibiotic resistant than before.

3. Antibiotics are given to animals as a preventive measure. This creates a strong selective pressure for resistant bacteria, as well as leakages (of antibiotic) into the subsequent meat which people eat.

(3) Is also an ethical issue.

Species Diversity

Species diversity is the diversity of species in a community. Put simply, how many different species are there in a community? Five or 5,000? Which has the higher diversity? Not rocket science I hope.

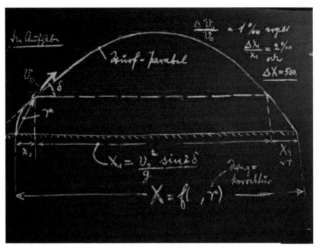

Rocket science... Maybe

That's some rocket science, I don't really know what it is, but I don't wish to find out, and neither do you. Just a little motivator to not complain about biology.

Now for a little talk about deforestation and agriculture. Deforestation is the removal of trees in forests, and agriculture is the cultivation of useful plants to people which are often carefully selected for, and occupy a large area by themselves (like corn).

It's not hard to figure out the impact both have on species diversity. Deforestation practically removes many, whole trees, and with them goes the shelter and food source of many other organisms. A great reduction in species diversity can be expected as a result.

Agriculture by humans results in a single dominant species which occupies vast land at the expense of others. Humans actively remove other species by the use of pesticides, insecticides and (indirectly) fertilisers. This, too, will lead to a great decrease in species diversity.

Index of Diversity

Species diversity is described as the number of species in a community. The more species, the higher the diversity. What if there are two separate communities like this:

Community #1 has 150 individuals per each of 20 different species (3000 individuals in total)

Community #2 has 10 individuals per each of 19 species, and 2990 individuals of the last species (3000 individuals in total)

It doesn't take a complex formula to figure out that community #1 is far more diverse compared to community #2, despite them having the same number of species and individuals. The distribution of individuals to species is important in determining a community's diversity.

The above example is easy enough, but for most purposes a formula is needed. This formula measures the index of diversity, which is simply a measure of diversity in a community. By calculating it and obtaining a numerical value, different communities can be easily compared.

Right, here it comes...

$$D = \frac{N(N-1)}{\sum n(n-1)}$$

No, don't run away yet! Wait and see how easy it is to work out.

D = Diversity index

N = total number of all organisms

n = total number of organisms of each species

Σ = sum of

Now it's simply a matter of replacing numbers. Look, I made it all purple so you would enjoy looking at it. Let's work out the index of diversity for community #1.

Firstly, we need a value for N. What's the total number of organisms? 3000. Sorted.

Next, we need a value for N - 1. No calculators! ...2999, sorted.

Finally, we need a value for n and n - 1. n = 150, while n - 1 = 149.

Drawing up a table helps:

species	n	n - 1	n(n - 1)
a	150	149	22350
b	150	149	22350
c	150	149	22350
d	150	149	22350
e	150	149	22350
f	150	149	22350
g	150	149	22350
h	150	149	22350
i	150	149	22350
j	150	149	22350
k	150	149	22350
l	150	149	22350
m	150	149	22350
n	150	149	22350
o	150	149	22350
p	150	149	22350
q	150	149	22350
r	150	149	22350
s	150	149	22350
t	150	149	22350
Total	**3000**	**2980**	**447000**

$$\text{So, D} = \frac{3000 * 2999}{447000} = \frac{8{,}997{,}000}{447000} = 20$$

20 in this case is maximum diversity (there are 20 different species). If the index were 1, then diversity would have been non-existent. An index of 10 would indicate moderate diversity.

Now work out the index of diversity for community #2 using the table above and the walk through as a guide. You should get a pretty low value. I know it's a bit confusing that the above numbers are identical in all the columns, but if you work out community #2 then the values for 1 species should be different to the other 19.

Most of the time all species will have different values. The working of it is the same though.

#OOTM3: HOW SMOKING IS DELETING YOUR Y...
by Ariana Explora
84 views · 5 months ago

#OOTM2: Neanderthals Were HUMANS? London Skyline...
by Ariana Explora
38 views · 6 months ago

#OOTM1: Is the X Chromosome Really a Sex...
by Ariana Explora
87 views · 7 months ago

Exam Preparation

How to: Nail Application Questions
by Ariana Explora
91 views · 5 months ago

MY CAMBRIDGE INTERVIEW EXPERIENCE
by Ariana Explora
1,123 views · 5 months ago

TOP 5 TIPS FOR A LEVEL BIOLOGY STUDENTS
by Ariana Explora
8,561 views · 6 months ago

Revision Videos

WHY CAN'T PHOTOSYNTHESIS GO ON...
Ariana Explora

The Cell Cycle Secret Language DECODED
by Ariana Explora

1000-Year Old Borough Market and LEARN...
by Ariana Explora

Find me on

Printed in Great Britain
by Amazon